How to Motivate People!

How to Motivate People!

The 3 Magic Keys to Unlock Anyone's Hidden Motivation

Lyn Kelley, Ph.D.
Edited by Robin Renna

iUniverse, Inc.
New York Lincoln Shanghai

How to Motivate People!
The 3 Magic Keys to Unlock Anyone's Hidden Motivation

iUniverse books may be ordered through booksellers or by contacting:

iUniverse
2021 Pine Lake Road, Suite 100
Lincoln, NE 68512
www.iuniverse.com
1-800-Authors (1-800-288-4677)

First Edition

ISBN-13: 978-0-595-38002-2 (pbk)
ISBN-13: 978-0-595-82373-4 (ebk)
ISBN-10: 0-595-38002-6 (pbk)
ISBN-10: 0-595-82373-4 (ebk)

Printed in the United States of America

This book is dedicated to my greatest motivator,
my daughter,

Kristin Anne Kelley

TABLE OF CONTENTS

of your progress. Most of the issues addressed, such as overcoming obstacles and breaking down goals into manageable steps, are ongoing issues that you will want to remain aware of as you continue to pursue your goals and dreams. Once you have learned the process of goal attainment, you can apply it throughout your life to all your other goals and life dreams. When in doubt, you can refer back to the steps outlined here and use them for guidance.

Becoming motivated is a *process* and is best achieved when following the steps in order as outlined in this book.

The goals of these exercises are several. First, they are designed to simplify and organize the process of motivation and goal planning—to make it an accessible process at which you can succeed. Second, they are designed to give you specific suggestions for ways in which to *choose* your goals and to pursue them. Third, they are designed to stress the overall importance of goal planning and organization, to make you realize how much more satisfying your life can be when you stick with your goals and see them through. Completing these exercises is *your first step* in becoming motivated to achieve your goals. And, if you have read this far, all you need to do is keep going, ***one step at a time.***

—Nothin' to it, but to do it!

—Lyn Kelley

Part I:

HOW TO MOTIVATE YOURSELF

—All our dreams can come true—if we have the courage to pursue them.
                                                    —Walt Disney

Theories of Motivation—
Which One Fits You?

Motivation can be defined in different terms according to different psychological theories. Some of these theories are described in brief:

Psychoanalytic theory states that motivation represents the pursuit to fulfill repressed needs and drives. The *goal* is "fulfillment and self knowledge." Freud contributed greatly to the field of motivational change by defining his *pleasure principle*. He believed that motivation is governed by the tendency to seek pleasure and avoid pain. People generally will be much more motivated (and act much more quickly) to avoid pain. Once they are in a "comfort zone" they will move diligently toward pleasure. Jung's motivational theory is based on consciousness-raising—the individual's innate need to uncover the "self"—one's true, authentic being.

From a *behavioral* standpoint, motivation is expressed in terms of physical drives: desires and needs. The *goal* is "to get what we want." The major premise of leading behaviorist B.F. Skinner's work was, "we do what we do because of what happens to us when we do it."

Existential theory discusses motivation in terms of the person's innate need for meaning. The *goal* is meaning and purpose, or "a reason to live." Victor Frankl's study of Holocaust survivors (1992) revealed man's meaning was primarily social interdependency. Alfred Adler believed that all our drives have a purpose—to feel important—to move us from a feeling of minus to a feeling of plus.

Scientific theory focuses more on intrinsic motivation and defines it in terms of innate curiosity. The *goal* is "to know." People who are drawn to the fields of science and technology are motivated by this theory.

The *social or systemic* theory of motivation can be defined in relation to societal pressures, to the surrounding people who exert influence and thus define the terms of motivation. Thus the *goal* is "acceptance and approval." Alfred Adler felt strongly that people could not be studied in isolation, but only in terms of social context. We are motivated by the effect we will have on others. It is important to note here that many people are conflicted about which "society" to seek approval in. For example, a teenager may want peer acceptance more than family acceptance, or may want a certain peer group acceptance more than another one.

Cognitive-behavioral theory states that the primary factor involved in motivation is feeling in control of one's situation rather than being controlled by external agents. Also important are autonomy, a sense of competence, and perceived self-efficacy. The goals are self-determination and freedom. In several studies (1977), Bandura tested the role of self-efficacy as it related to motivation and demonstrated that an individual's *belief* about his or her ability to accomplish an activity directly affected performance. If a person believes that he/she is capable of succeeding at something, he/she has a much greater chance of performing well at that activity or task. Thus, ability is not fixed but depends on self-perception.

Humanistic theory believes that motivation entails the journey toward self-actualization. The psychologist Abraham Maslow (1970) is credited with the "needs hierarchy" that is referred to throughout psychology and self help books. He believed that as the lower levels of needs are satisfied, people move up the hierarchy of needs ladder. The *goal* of self-actualization is that of reaching a state in which one feels fulfilled in life and can live in the present moment (see exercise 1:1).

1. *Level one* of the hierarchy represents the most basic needs—to survive and stay alive.

2. *Level two* is the need for safety, security and protection.

3. *Level three* is the need to be social—to respond, communicate, love and belong.

4. *Level four* is the need for self esteem—to respect oneself and receive respect from others.

5. *Level five* is the need for self–actualization—to be creative, to imagine, to self–motivate, to realize one's full potential.

Spiritual/New Thought is not really a theory, but a belief system, and warrants mention here. As mentioned previously, motivation is largely values-based. The idea is that you will be motivated most by what you truly believe in—what is most important to you. Your personal values are *who you are* deep down. It is your core, your soul, your spirit, the God within you, your innermost self, your *true, authentic self.* Your life force, or *chi,* is what causes you to survive, to create, to procreate, to produce, to care for and to love. When you are "living who you are" you will be your most motivated self.

As you can see, we have an abundance of scientifically, psychologically and spiritually based theories. While these were the predominate theories in our research, there are many more. Although my emphasis is on humanistic, spiritual and cognitive-behavioral theories, each of these theories has legitimacy, and it is possible to support many or all of them. This book utilizes an integrated approach.

Abraham Maslow (1970), the great humanistic psychologist, said there are two types of motivation, *deficiency motivation* and *growth motivation*. *Deficiency motivation* is the desire to fill a perceived void in one's life, particularly a basic need such as food, water, air, shelter, or warmth. *Growth motivation* is the desire to improve one's life, after all the basic needs and comforts have been met. This book focuses predominantly on *growth motivation*.

Growth motivation is really what I call *achievement motivation* There are several elements to keep in mind. One, which I've already discussed, is the difference between *intrinsic* and *extrinsic* motivation—namely, whether one is motivated because of an inherent curiosity and desire for knowledge or productivity (intrinsic), or because of pressure exerted from the outside, such as from teachers, employers, and family members (extrinsic). Another factor is a person's value system, which I have already discussed. A third issue is that there are several *phases*, or steps, of motivation. All of the following phases need to be considered when assessing the whole process of motivation:

- Determining what motivates you
- Deciding on a goal
- Implementing a course of action that leads toward that goal
- Commitment to the goal and course of action
- Persisting in one's quest of the goal over a period of time and in the face of difficulties, obstacles and setbacks
- Achieving the goal successfully
- Maintaining the success over time

—You only get as far in the world as your desires are high.
                                                                    —Mark Victor Hansen

What is Success, Really?

Success can be defined in a number of ways, depending on who is defining it, his or her perspective, and the type of activity being evaluated. Success for a student who is math-phobic may mean passing calculus and never having to take another math class, whereas success for a student who excels in math and hopes to attend MIT may mean getting an A+ in the same calculus course. Success can be defined by external criteria such as money, fame, love, recognition, and by internal criteria such as fulfillment, happiness and peace, or a combination of the two. If you are trying to motivate someone else, it is important to understand that person's definition of success and perhaps encourage them to broaden these definitions to include more attainable goals and standards.

External criteria are factors such as material wealth and the perceptions of others. In this regard, success might mean earning more than $100,000 dollars a year or receiving an award as Outstanding Teacher of the Year. External criteria are influenced by one's culture: success may be defined very differently in Kenyan culture and Thai culture—or even in the cultures of Northern California and New England. Internally defined criteria consist of one's own perceptions and definitions of success. Internal criteria may consist of satisfaction of goal fulfillment, a feeling of accomplishment and a sense of meaning in one's purpose in life. My definition of success is simply "doing who you are." (Just as long as "who you are" isn't hurting anyone else.)

What I have learned from helping clients either in coaching or psychotherapy is that most people are in some level of denial about their life satisfaction. One of the first steps to getting motivated is to *acknowledge that you definitely need or want improvement in some area.* The following exercises are designed to assist you in determining your current satisfaction level in your life. Once you have determined the areas that you are not satisfied with, you will be able to set goals around improving those areas.

The question of whether internal or external motivation produces more effective and/or longer lasting results is the subject of ongoing debate, and many theorists are now stressing the interrelation of the two types. Jung's work focuses on integration of both the "ego" (external) and the "self" (internal). Also, it has been shown that as one pursues a goal for extrinsic reasons, the motivation often transfers into intrinsic needs. Thus, what starts out simply as a desire for a material thing, can evolve, over the course of time, into a part of the person's being, or core self. For example, a teenage boy who gets a part-time job at an auto garage to make some extra money for a car, finds out that he loves working on cars. He then enters full-time training as an auto mechanic and loves his work.

Your values, those things most important to you, will also have an effect on your motivation. Is it more important to you to be very wealthy or to have free time to pursue family or hobbies? If your answer is "free time," then you would be more motivated to attain a sales quota at work if your boss offered you a day off rather than a bonus. For the person who values wealth, the bonus would be a more motivating reward. Therefore, it is vitally important to understand what you (or others) value most in life.

In summary, the main points in determining what your level of motivation will be are:

- How you feel about your goal in relation to self, others and your environment during the pursuit, attainment, and post-attainment of goals

- Whether your goal is what YOU want, or what you think OTHERS want for you

- Your goals take into account your well-being, as well as the well-being of others, and of society

- Your goals are "optimally challenging"—realistic—attainable—neither too easy or too difficult

- Your goals have a holistic framework—consider your overall health during pursuit of goals

- Your goals are congruent with your core values and are prioritized, yet, flexible

- Your goals bring up passion, desire, joy

- Attainment of your goals causes you to feel validated and empowered

---

—I think the purpose of life is to do something that contributes and helps you to touch people beyond our lifetime. I think the purpose of life is to do something that will outlast it.

—Anthony Robbins

Exercise 1:1
Maslow's "Hierarchy of Needs" Diagram and Exercise

The psychologist Abraham Maslow asserted that people are motivated to satisfy basic needs. Level one represents the most basic needs. As the lower levels of needs are satisfied, people move up the hierarchy of needs ladder.

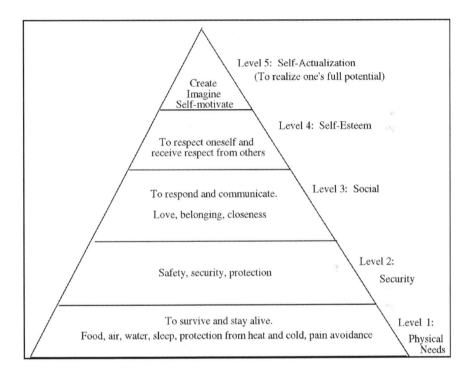

Circle the needs you feel are met in your life right now. Add any other needs and goals that apply to your life in the appropriate boxes above.

On which level or levels of the hierarchy are you now?

What can you do to further satisfy the higher levels of the hierarchy?

—*Human behavior flows from three main sources: desire, emotion and knowledge.*

—Plato

Exercise 1:2
Life Satisfaction Rating

Place a number between 1 and 10 next to each area of your life, with 10 being the most satisfied and happy. Not all categories will apply to you. Feel free to add more categories that may fit for you. Repeat this rating every few months to see if your life is improving.

	<u>Date</u>	<u>Date</u>	<u>Date</u>	<u>Date</u>
Love Relationships:				
Friends/Social:				
Family:				
Physical Health/Appearance:				
Emotional/Mental Health:				
Spiritual Health/Peace:				
Career:				
Finances:				
Home/Living Space:				
Hobbies/Recreation:				
Education/Learning:				
Productivity/Creativity:				
Other:				

> —*The whole point of being alive is to evolve into the complete person you were intended to be.*
>
> —Oprah Winfrey

Chapter Two:
What Do I Want?

How to Know What You Really, Really Want

Before you can "go for your goals," "do it now," or "make it happen," it is important to determine what it is you really want. As our world becomes more progressive, and people become more educated and more sophisticated, we have many more choices than ever before. Our great grandparents had very few choices. Our grandparents had slightly more choices. Our parents had a few more choices. We have many more than they did.

First, you have to decide on a goal. That being said, you need to know that you have the right to change your mind at any time, modify your goal, or decide on a completely different goal. Changing goals and directions often has consequences however. Usually change requires a temporary setback. However, most people do change over time, and as we get to know more about who we really are, our goals often change as well. This is a part of growing and evolving.

Many of us have what is called goal conflict. You may not even realize you have goal conflict—you are either trying to achieve too much at once, or you want too many different things and cannot start any one thing due to your confusion. Sometimes goal conflict arises out of our need for perfection. Many people have a need to do all things well, and complete lots of lofty goals in a short period of time. This is known as the "Type E" personality. This is a person who feels they need to be "everything" to "everybody." The Type E personality is very similar to co-dependency. When you are trying to be too perfect, life will be a constant disappointment, because no one can ever be perfect. In fact we cannot even get close. Trying to do too much is also known as "over-functioning." When you are over-doing you will eventually get burned out. This will not serve you or anyone else. Therefore, I encourage you to choose your goals carefully, and take the pressure off of yourself by only working on a few goals at a time. You will find in later chapters lots of tips for staying balanced and sane while pursuing your goals.

Next, you have to *take action* on your goals. If you state that you have a goal, but have not yet taken any action toward it, you need to figure out why. Either you don't really desire this goal enough or you have obstacles that are getting in your way. Part II of this book discusses these obstacles, both real and perceived. Once you have completed the exercises in Part II, you should either begin taking some action on your stated goals, or consider changing your goals!

—Some of the biggest problems arise when we begin to believe that we are perfect, or that the world should be perfect.

—Leo Buscaglia

Why Choosing the Right Goal is Your "Power Button"

It is important *first* to "sift through the muck" and determine what it is you really want, and what it is you can actually do at this time toward attaining it. Goals are values-based. The best way to resolve goal conflict is to take time to study your personal value system (see Exercise 2:1). It is extremely important to choose the right goals for you, as the goal itself will serve as a "power button" to motivate you and propel you forward. When obstacles and challenges try to bring you down, focusing on your goal and seeing yourself at the finish line will carry you through.

Second, your goal may not be a healthy one. Healthy goals are those that take into account your overall well being in addition to the well-being of others. Sometimes our goals or desires are self-defeating. You may be motivated to pursue jobs or relationships, but the jobs or relationships that you pursue are destructive to your well-being and in the end will hinder rather than further your aims. You need to explore your underlying motives for the goal and discuss them with the people in your life who you trust in order to determine whether the goal is a healthy one that should be pursued (see Exercise 2:2).

We need to explore all areas of our lives and strive for health and balance in mental, physical, emotional, spiritual, interpersonal and professional areas. Realistic and healthy goals will complement the rest of an individual's lifestyle, will mesh with the individual's other goals, and will therefore serve to build self-esteem. Your goals must correlate with your interests, value system, and life-goals in order to be meaningful to you in the long run.

The *third* element to consider is whether or not your goals are realistic and attainable. To be optimally motivated, your goals should correspond to your level of expertise and be able to be completed in a manageable time frame. Unlike a wish or fantasy, a goal must be *attainable*. Thus, for a person who began playing the violin at age 30, playing in a string quartet at a friend's marriage is a more realistic goal than becoming concert master of the Berlin Philharmonic. A person who wishes to run a marathon but has bad knees, should consider that this activity may not only be unattainable but may be self destructive as well.

Fourth, I need to mention the influence of greed in determining your goals. There is a continuum between being overly giving and accommodating on one end, and overly greedy and self centered on the other end. Neither end is a healthy place. If your goals are too self focused and self accumulating they will not be satisfying or meaningful in the long run. The person who acts to amass an empire will often destroy relationships or their own mental and/or physical health in the process. I have seen many extremely selfish people get what they want, only to be left with no one but themselves. The saying, "It's lonely at the top," is only true if you have been self centered and selfish along the way. Ask yourself these questions: 1) Will my goals, once achieved, contribute to the world in a meaningful way? 2) Will my pursuit of my goals cause distress to others? 3) Will my pursuit of my goals alienate me from friends and family? And 4) How will I feel once I've achieved my goals?

> —*The penalty of a selfish attempt to make the world confer a living without contributing to the progress or happiness of mankind is generally a failure to the individual. The pity is that when he goes down, he inflicts heartache and misery also on others who are in no way responsible.*
>
> —John D. Rockefeller

The Optimal Challenge

As we pointed out in Chapter One, Bandura's tests demonstrated that if a person *believes* that he/she is capable of succeeding at something, he/she has a much greater chance of performing well at that activity or task. Moreover, a sense of *self-efficacy* can be fostered by setting attainable goals—ones that are neither too large nor too distant. In his study, Deci (1985) defined such goals as "optimally challenging." Success on these small goals fosters a greater intrinsic motivation for related activities, and can thus eventually lead to the achievement of larger goals for which the smaller ones were stepping stones. Moreover, the more attractive the goal is to you, the better your performance is likely to be, so it is important that the goal you select is one you have some *passion* about.

The dilemma is exemplified in the case of top athletes who sacrifice everything to train in their sport. This single-minded focus pays off when they make it to the Olympics and perhaps even win a medal. However, the dangers of this narrow focus are revealed when the Olympics are over. Many athletes have attested to undergoing periods of severe depression after retiring from their sport. Because they have neglected academics, family, friends, and hobbies, they are suddenly confronted with a void and question their ability to pursue a new and unrelated goal of perhaps a less overwhelming nature. The other danger of pursuing one goal to the exclusion of all others is that one's whole sense of self rests on this one success. Should one fail, or even perform only at a mediocre level, it is easy to internalize this assessment as one that reflects on one's whole character rather than merely this one activity.

Our society tends to pedestalize "over-achievers" referring to them as "ambitious," and "driven." However, studies show that over-achievers are at just as much of a disadvantage as under-achievers. They score themselves as just as unhappy on happiness scales. They are just as frustrated, just as lonely, and have about the same levels of self esteem as underachievers. In *Life's Too Short!*, Abraham Twerski (1997) writes, "The goal of changing the self-concept [of a narrowly-focused overachiever] to a positive one is not to convert an ambitious person into a beachcomber, but to allow the person to perform at the same level without jeopardizing his or her physical and emotional health."

PPPP Principle that Will Propel You Beyond Belief

The "PPPP" principle is a powerful tool to assist you in determining what you really want and staying on your path. It stands for *prophesy, passion, power,* and *propulsion.* The first part is *prophesy* which is essentially your "vision" of the dream you would like to create in your life. Visualization involves picturing certain things in one's mind. Try to visualize yourself actually doing your goal, living your goal, succeeding in your goal. Describe exactly what that looks like, from beginning to end. This could take you an hour, or even longer. Do not be tempted to skip this exercise. If you cannot visualize yourself actually achieving your goal, this will be a major obstacle to your success! On the other hand, if you can visualize yourself actually achieving the goal, this will provide the *passion* you need to continue to do the work involved. *Passion* then creates *power,* which *propels* you into full action.

Visualization involves picturing certain things in your mind. Actually we are constantly visualizing. Visualization is a technique for bringing about healing and change. It works by bringing subconscious mental and emotional patterns into consciousness.

For example, a man loves baseball, but suffers from arthritis in his hip. Before going to a baseball camp, the man visualizes himself playing baseball, feeling limber and free. In minute detail he fantasizes his movement, his performance, his emotional experience, exactly as he wants it to be. He sees and feels himself a winner. The man proceeds to have a wonderful time at camp and experiences no pain while playing baseball.

Picture the fulfillment of your goals: see it, hear it, smell it, touch it, taste it. Think about what your life will be like when the goals are completed; what will be different, how you will feel. Afterwards, describe the picture in writing.

Passion is born out of our visions. True happiness and inner peace can only be found by pursuing our passion. We can have passion for many different things in our lives, from enjoyment of an athletic sport to finding a cure for a specific disease. Passion can be about how we want to feel (loved, admired), how much we want to have (money, material things), how well we want to do (win, improve), how much fun we want to have (hobbies, entertainment), or any number of things. Perhaps you have many passions. If so, one might say you are a "passionate person." Having passion simply means that you have been able to express your inner desires outwardly and have your desires manifested into action and emotion.

Your passion is your purpose and when you suppress (or allow others to suppress) your passion, you hurt yourself. The price you pay for not living your life purpose is huge. The price you pay for not pursuing your dreams is huge. The price you pay for not achieving your goals is huge. You pay the price in self esteem, personal satisfaction, self actualization and fulfillment. That's a price you can't afford to pay.

—*Success is not the result of spontaneous combustion. You must set yourself on fire.*

—Reggie Leach

Exercise 2:1
Values Clarification

What are Values?

Values can be defined in a variety of ways. The dictionary gives the all-inclusive definition, "something (as a principle or quality) intrinsically valuable or desirable." Values involve personal choice, and when assessing your values it is important to be honest with yourself. Values reflect human qualities and lifestyle qualities that are important to you.

Common Societal Values

> Children, religion, ethics, good physical health, good mental health, family stability, close friends, independence, saving for the future, honesty, equality, justice, education, knowledge, maturity, loyalty, obedience, safety, peace of mind, beauty, originality, tradition, love, wealth, power, success, fame, respect for authority, freedom of choice, community service, world peace, the environment…

Think about which of these values (and what others) are important to you. Write them down, then try to put them in order of priority to you.

> —*The strongest principle of growth lies in human choice.*
> —George Eliot

Exercise 2:2
Why Do I Want It?
Assessing Personal Values

1. What are your main values in life?

2. What past experience was the most painful for you?

3. What past experience brought you the most joy?

4. What pain do you not want yourself or others ever to feel?

5. What joy do you not want yourself or others to do without?

6. What comes naturally to you that gives you an unfair advantage?

7. When do you feel so immersed in something that you forget that the rest of the world exists?

8. If you could do anything in the world that you wanted to, what would it be?

9. When did you accomplish something that you feel very good about?

10. How would you like to see your world?

—And now here is my secret, a very simple secret; it is only with the heart that one can see rightly, what is essential is invisible to the eye.
—Antoine de Saint-Exupery

Exercise 2:3
As a Child I...

Sit quietly for 15 to 30 minutes and think back to when you were a child at different ages. Write everything you can remember about what you liked doing, who you liked being with, and what you would do with your day when no one told you what you had to do, should do, or needed to do.

After you have brainstormed everything you can think of, look over your list and see if there are any general themes. For example my general themes were the outdoors and nature, animals, building and creating, playing with friends, sports, reading and writing. My personality themes were appreciative, shy, generous, serious, long attention span, self conscious, competitive, easy going, organized and mechanical.

Age 1—5 (Before school years):

Age 5—8 (Early childhood):

Age 9—12 (Late childhood):

Age 12—14 (Early adolescence):

—*I want to do it because I want to do it.*

—Amelia Earhart

Exercise 2:4
What Do I Want?
Steps to Decisions

1. Define a particular problem, question, or choice with which you are struggling:

2. List your options for resolving the question or choice:

3. Write the possible outcomes for each option:
   (It may help at this stage to consult books and/or experts for more information)

4. Write the pros and cons for each option:

5. Talk with 3 supportive/trusted people about the options and write down useful suggestions:
   (It may be tempting to skip this step, but in fact this is one of the *most valuable* steps).

6. Determine which option corresponds most closely with your overall values and goals:

7. Determine which option is the healthiest for all involved:

8. Make a decision that you can commit to for a specified period of time:

—Make careful decisions and then pull the trigger.

—Dr. Phil McGraw

Chapter Three:
How People REALLY Change

The Fallacy of Willpower

As we have discussed earlier, there are a variety of factors and forces that can cause a person to create self change. There are internal forces, as well as external forces. People change to avoid pain and/or to seek pleasure. People can change from a single thought, emotion, catharsis, event, idea, statement, experience or decision. Sometimes people change because they *want* to; sometimes they change because they *have* to.

There is a myth that most people believe, that all it takes is willpower. Many people believe that change or action is simply "mind over matter." This is partly true, in the sense that once you have made the decision to change or act, there will be many difficulties to work through along the way. Sometimes getting through the tough times does require a tremendous amount of willpower or "true grit." Sometimes you just have to "gut it out." However, your greatest motivators are your commitment and passion for the result. As mentioned previously, aside from what you inherit genetically, there are three main factors in motivation—values, enjoyment and empowerment. You will be moved by what you value, enjoy, and for what you receive the greatest validation.

A recent study reported that when Americans were asked if they would keep their current job if they won the lottery. A surprising 22% said they would. When business owners were asked if they would keep running their businesses, an amazing 47% said they would. This means that when a person is truly happy and satisfied with their work, they would keep doing it even if they didn't need the money. Therefore, there must be more to work than simply willpower. Most people actually thrive on overcoming challenges and achieving something they feel is important.

—*I discovered I always have choices and sometimes it's only a choice of attitude.*

—Judith M. Knowlton

Pain vs. Pleasure—Who Wins?

B.F. Skinner said, "People do what they do because of what happens to them when they do it." What causes most people to change is either the fear of punishment or the hope of reward. When your desired outcome is great enough, you will be motivated to act. Therefore, your hopes and dreams must stir excitement inside you in order to give you that extra push. We are first motivated to be free of pain and discomfort. Then we are motivated for life improvement. The motivation for self-improvement and personal growth is to be happier and more satisfied.

The motivation for any change is to make your life better or to make you *feel* better. If a person perceives making a change as positive, one that will improve the quality of life and bring about feelings of pleasure, this will begin to provide the motivation to make the change. If, however, a person perceives the work involved in making changes as outweighing the desired outcome, then motivation will decline. For example, if one has an item to return to a store that is far away from home or work (10–15 miles), one would need to decide whether the amount of money that he/she would get back is worth the amount of time and energy the process would involve. The more work (pain) that is associated with the change process, the less motivation the person will generally have. This pain-pleasure principle controls our motivation.

For most people, the fear of loss is much greater than the desire for gain. One need only look at the plethora of advertisements geared toward pain prevention to confirm this insight. The typical cycle of dieting manifests the force of the pain/pleasure principle. The diet begins as a result of the pain associated with being overweight: a person looks in the mirror and thinks, "I can't stand how I look" or "I'm worried about my health." Then the person begins the diet by gaining education about different diets, cutting out certain foods, etc. As changes are made, the person begins to lose weight and as a result begins to feel better about his/her looks, to have more energy, and to feel healthier. The pleasure derived from this immediate success is very motivating, but soon the person notices that the weight loss is slowing down and he/she begins to feel discouraged. In addition, the person encounters unrelated problems at work or in a relationship that adds stress and pain. As the pleasure associated with the diet dwindles, and the diet proves to be powerless to affect the new sources of pain, the person loses motivation, binges, gains back a pound, decides the diet is too much work, and quits.

In attempting to make a change, it is helpful to determine whether you are typically more motivated by alleviating pain or pursuing pleasure. To help you determine this, ask yourself the question, "What does my work mean to me?" Did you reply, "It provides me with the money to have a great lifestyle?" If your answer to this is "yes", you are probably more motivated by seeking pleasure. If you responded, "It keeps me from being poor and unable to pay my bills," you are probably more motivated by avoiding pain. This is an important determination, as it may help you to devise a more effective strategy to overcome hurdles when you come to an impasse. At difficult times it may be more helpful to tell yourself something like, "I need to make sure I don't go back to that place where I couldn't pay my bills," rather than, "I must keep moving forward so that I can pay for the children's college education."

—*There are only two stimulants to one's best efforts: the fear of punishment, and the hope of reward.*

—John M. Wilson

Quick Change vs. Gradual Change

People can change many aspects of themselves *instantly* and with relative ease, such as quitting drinking "cold turkey." People can change just by making a decision with a snap of their fingers. There are many psychological modalities that purport their ability to help people make immediate changes in their lives. Eriksonian hypnosis and neurolinguistic programming (NLP) are two of the most common. NLP, for example, can help people eliminate a lifetime phobia in less than an hour—something that in traditional therapies could take five years to work through.

However, according to acclaimed change researcher James Prochaska, Professor of Psychology and Director of the Cancer Prevention Research Center at the University of Rhode Island in Kingston, there are over 300 therapeutic modalities being used by psychotherapists today. According to his research, not one of the over 400 modalities is more successful at bringing about change than a determined individual working on his/her own. The key word here is *determined*.

The only problem with instantaneous changes is that many of them do not last. This is primarily due to the fact that we are "creatures of habit." Although people can change in an instant, most people need long term reinforcement or continuous support to keep the changes in place. However, many of these techniques can be incorporated into longer-term programs. Coaching, mentoring, sponsoring or counseling has shown to be extremely valuable when it comes to long term change.

People are creatures of habit, and as a result, change is difficult. Change is usually a gradual process that consists of many small steps. Often, you are slowly working your way towards a goal without even realizing it. According to Prochaska (1995), "The average person makes the same New Year's resolution three years in a row before actually accomplishing it". While many people can change quickly, Prochaska has found that people rarely make sudden, dramatic shifts from one behavior to another. Instead, he has found that most people pass through a series of well-defined stages:

1) Pre-contemplation

2) Contemplation

3) Preparation

4) Action

5) Maintenance/Support

6) Termination/Relapse

In his book *Changing for Good*, Prochaska (1995) explains that one may require several passes through these steps before succeeding. In fact, he equates the process of change to that of a "spiraling upward", or of climbing the Leaning Tower of Pisa—first, you walk up, but as you approach the lower part of each floor, you begin to head down. A few steps later you resume your ascent.

Many "change programs" have been unsuccessful because they failed to realize the importance of the preparation stages. It would be nice start right away on your "action plan." However, if you are willing to take the time to get to know yourself better first, you will be much more successful. You also will be more likely to stay on your path rather than do a lot of starting and stopping and changing. These stops and changes are major setbacks on your road to success.

—Nothing can stop the man with the right mental attitude from achieving his goal; nothing on earth can help the man with the wrong mental attitude.

—Thomas Jefferson

What You Can Change and What You Can't

Not everything can be changed. Most of our physical qualities cannot be changed, although they can be altered through artificial means, or, in some cases, manipulated by exercise, diet, or the intake of chemicals. An excellent study on this subject has been done by Martin Seligman, in his book *What You Can Change and What You Can't* (1994). Seligman discusses the term "human plasticity," or the ability to change. Those characteristics that are difficult (if not impossible) to change are called "heritable." Those characteristics that are easier to change are called "changeable."

Seligman contrasts the enduring historical belief that one's role is determined by class, gender, family profession, God's will, etc., with the belief that one's role is determined by individual drive, character and self-determination. Nonetheless, there is still a wide range of attitudes toward the power of self-determination. There is a continuum between the two extremes of total self will and total fate. Fate can also be defined as "destiny" or "God's will." It is useful also to find out where you stand on the self-determination spectrum: Are you waiting for divine intervention to solve your problems, or do you think you have absolute control over your actions? The optimal goal is of course a healthy combination that rests on gaining insight into what can genuinely be controlled by the individual and what cannot. Once this is understood, you can concentrate your energy on developing attainable goals.

Interestingly, this balance is reflected in the recitation used by Alcoholics Anonymous: "God grant me the serenity to accept the things I cannot change, the courage to change the things I can, and the wisdom to know the difference." The saying combines the belief in a higher power with the belief in self-determination. The centrality of this combination to the AA philosophy is perhaps a partial explanation for the organization's astounding popularity and endurance.

There has been much debate in the scientific community and in society as a whole about *nature* vs. *nurture*. Perhaps the most effective work that has been done in attempting to determine which traits are heritable and which are changeable has been done with identical twins reared apart. What scientists have determined from these studies is that the most heritable traits (aside from physical characteristics) are:

1) IQ
2) Mental speed

3) Alcohol and drug abuse

4) Natural weight

5) Crime and conduct

6) Job choice

7) Cheerfulness or depression.

However, all of these can be altered to some extent. According to Seligman, recent studies show that IQ has an approximate heritability degree of .75. This means that 25% of our IQ comes from our actions and our experiences. The general consensus within the scientific and psychological communities now is that personality has approximately a .50 heritability degree. This opens the door for much opportunity for self-improvement.

—Great dancers are not great because of their technique; they are great because of their passion.

—Martha Graham

Get Fed Up!

When I did research for this book, I asked all my friends and relatives "What motivates you?" I got a variety of answers, but one that kept coming up was "anger." People said that they won't change until they get mad enough, frustrated enough, or "fed up." For some this means "hitting bottom." Anger is a strong emotion. Anger can create passion. One must be careful about anger, however. While anger is a normal, useful emotion, it can be self-destructive if allowed to go too far or out of control.

The most important thing about anger is to recognize it early on. You need to get out of denial about your anger, and ask yourself what you are angry about. If you deny your anger it will get pent up. Pent up anger is like a pressure cooker. It gets stronger and stronger until one (often tiny) thing will set it off and it will blow. Blowing up is always self-destructive and/or other-destructive.

On the other hand, many people never blow up, they just hold anger in and turn it against themselves. Depression is anger turned inward. Depression causes fatigue and loss of motivation. Therefore, it is extremely important that you become aware of your anger and frustration before it turns against you.

Anger can be used as a powerful motivator if used in a positive way. Anger is important because it warns us and protects us from hurt and pain. Here's how to use anger as a positive motivating force. First, you need to take some time each day to meditate or relax and ask yourself if you are angry about anything in your life. If so, you need to put it into words to yourself, for example, "I'm angry when my teenager asks me for rides at the last minute." Second, you need to determine how you can and will set limits with yourself or others in order to handle your anger effectively. Third, you need to state your new limit (or commitment) to yourself and to others if they are involved. For example, you might say to yourself "I will no longer give rides to my teenager unless I get at least 10 hours advanced notice and it is convenient for me." Then you might say to your teenager, "I will no longer give you a ride unless I get at least 10 hours advanced notice, and then only if it is convenient for me."

There is a famous line in a movie where a man yells out the window of his apartment, *"I'm mad as hell and I'm not going to take it any more!"* This can be a life-changing statement. Simply stating aloud that you are FED UP and have reached your limit is very powerful. If anger motivates you, use it in a positive way and it will be your friend.

—It is easy to fly into a passion—anybody can do that—but to be angry with the right person to the right extent and at the right time and with the right object and in the right way—that is not easy, and it is not everyone who can do it.

—Aristotle

The Power of Commitment

For change to be lasting there needs to be a strong level of *commitment.* Commitment is what transforms a promise, hope, dream or goal into reality. If you are serious about achieving your goals, dreams and desires, you must *commit* to them one hundred percent. How do you develop this kind of total commitment or "definiteness of purpose," as Napoleon Hill calls it? You need to make achievement of your goals a *must.* It MUST be a MUST. You must move past wishful thinking such as, "it would be nice if…" and "I would love it if…" and "my life would be great if…" You must move on to "mustful" thinking. If you cannot "muster" up a "must" attitude about your goal, it probably isn't a very passionate one. If there's no passion, what's the point? Keep it as a wish or fantasy if you'd like, but just be aware that it is just a wish and not a goal.

Many people fear commitment because they think it will restrict them or shut them in. We would like to have options. We want freedom to make our own choices and change our minds whenever we want. We are reluctant to make verbal commitments for fear people will hold us to that standard and be disappointed in us if we do not live up to it. Here is the irony in commitment: commitment brings freedom! Commitment to your higher purpose brings you focus, power & freedom. You will become free of obligations and barriers that once got in your way. You will become free of self-sabotages. You will become free of binds, confusion and ambivalence. Making a commitment actually frees you up to be yourself and live more fully. You are much more likely to get the life of your dreams when you make and keep commitments!

Ask yourself these three questions about your commitments:

1. What three things am I most committed to in my life?
2. How are these commitments aligned with my higher purpose?
3. What did I do today that supports my commitments?

—You cannot claim commitment unless you take action. Have your actions be about your commitments.

—Lyn Kelley

Exercise 3:1
What Can I Change About Myself?

Make a list of your 10 most positive traits. Next to this trait, place an "I" if you think you inherited it. Place an "L" if you think you learned it from your environment. Place a "C" next to the trait if you feel this trait did not come naturally for you and you had to work on changing yourself in order to have it. (You may check more than one letter.)

Trait	I	L	C
1.			
2.			
3.			
4.			
5.			
6.			
7.			
8.			
9.			
10.			

Make a list of your 10 most negative traits, or things you would like to change about yourself. Next to this trait, place an "I" if you think you inherited it. Place an "L" if you think you learned it from your environment. Place a "C" next to the trait if you think you could change this trait if you really wanted to.

<u>Trait</u>	<u>I</u>	<u>L</u>	<u>C</u>
1.			
2.			
3.			
4.			
5.			
6.			
7.			
8.			
9.			
10.			

Set a goal for changing at least one thing about yourself now:

> —*If one advances confidently in the direction of his dreams, and endeavors to live the life which he has imagined, he will meet with a success unexpected in common hours.*
>
> —Henry David Thoreau

Exercise 3:2
One Year to Live

Anthony Burgess, the author of *A Clockwork Orange*, was 40 years old when he learned that he had a brain tumor that would kill him within a year. He had no money to leave his wife. He always knew that he had it in him to be a writer but he had never written a book. For the sole purpose of leaving behind royalties to his family, he began to write. He finished 5 ½ novels during the next year. Amazingly, his cancer went into remission and eventually disappeared. He went on to write and publish more than 70 books. Without his death sentence, he might never have written at all.

There is a "knowing" inside each of us about what our true gifts and talents are. Unfortunately, sometimes it takes a crisis to bring this knowledge forth. What would you do to bring forth your true self if you found out you only had one year to live? What are your hidden talents that have never been tested?

—Nothing will ever be attempted if all possible objections must be first overcome.

—Samuel Johnson

Chapter Four:
Access Your Greatness through Visioning

Your Personal Vision

George Lucas, creator of the *Star Wars* movies once said, "Great achievers are people of vision." Stephen Spielberg is another great visionary. A vision is a mental picture of what you want to create. Once you've created a vision of something, observe how it makes you feel. If it inspires you or excites you, you will be incited to action. Whenever you have a vision that makes you feel this way, be sure to write it down in as much detail as possible.

Your vision is what motivates you to set goals. Therefore, it is important to create a vision before attempting to set goals or create an action plan. Motivational experts call personal vision many different things, such as primary aim, main purpose, life mission, and core intention. The reason I prefer the term personal vision is that it implies a picture, and it is very helpful to create a picture of how your life will look when your mission is accomplished. Perhaps you don't have an end goal, but rather a process or life journey, and that is fine. Either way, it is important that you write out a statement and then either draw or describe a picture of your vision. Your personal vision predicates your mission.

—Every great achievement was a dream before someone of vision turned it into reality.

—Henry Kissinger

Your Mission Statement is
Your Vision Multiplied

It is extremely important to develop a *mission statement,* or *intention* for each area of your life in which you have goals to work on. Mission statements are intentions that arise out of one's values and vision. You can create specific goal statements with sub-goals, tasks and timelines from each mission statement. Thus, before goal-setting work can be done, it is important to define your vision and then to formulate it in terms of a mission. Determine your mission according to several criteria: the mission will have something to do with your value system, past experiences (either very negative or very positive), skills, talents, abilities, interests, and sources of joy. Finally, the mission will reflect your self-concept and perceptions about your ability to accomplish goals.

For example, my mission statement for this book is: *"I help people determine what they want, what they are willing to do to get it, motivate them and keep them on track until they have it."* The following is a list of the seven main areas of a person's life, and an example of a mission statement in each area:

Physical/Emotional Health: *"I am losing an average of one pound a week for the first 20 weeks of this year, and exercising at least 3 days a week."*

Relationship/Marriage: *"I am happily married and demonstrate love and respect for my spouse on a daily basis."*

Family: *"I spend at least one hour a day with my children doing something fun and/or interesting, uninterrupted."*

Professional/Career: *"I am a confident and successful real estate salesperson who lists and sells at least two homes per month."*

Social/Political: *"I belong to a business organization that contributes to the success of school-aged girls in the areas of science and math."*

Spiritual: *"I am an empowered woman who helps myself & others realize our own power and gifts, so we can ask for and receive all that we need and desire."*

Leisure/Recreation: *"I take golf lessons once a month and participate in a golf league that plays once or twice a week, both of which provide me with a lot of fun with enjoyable people."*

—Realize the power of your word. Your word is the power you have to create. It is a gift that comes directly from God.

—Don Miguel Ruiz

Exercise 4:1
My Personal Vision
Unfinished Sentences

Complete the following sentences as a method of clarifying what you value and what you want to accomplish:

1. On Saturday I like to_____.
2. If I had 24 hours to live I would_____.
3. If I had a million dollars I would_____.
4. I feel best when people_____.
5. In school I achieved_____.
6. The thing that I feel worst about in my education is_____.
7. I secretly wish that_____.
8. I like people who_____.
9. I feel proud of myself when_____.
10. I am embarrassed by_____.
11. I am trying to improve_____.
12. The hardest thing for me to do is_____.
13. I'll know I've "made it" when_____.
14. I want to learn to_____.
15. If I had to do it over again I would_____
16. Before I die I want to_____

—Keep your eyes on the stars and your feet on the ground.
                                        —Theodore Roosevelt

Exercise 4:2
Personal Mission Statement

Write your personal mission statement for each of the following areas:

1. Physical/Emotional Health

2. Relationship/Marriage

3. Family

4. Professional/Career

5. Financial

6. Social/Political

7. Spiritual

8. Hobbies/Recreation

—We first make our habits, and then our habits make us.
                                        —John Dryden

Chapter Five:
Goal Setting & Action Planning

Setting Goals that Leap You Into Action

Goals are born from vision. Denis Waitley, author *of The New Dynamics of Goal Setting* (1991), believes so strongly that people cannot succeed without goals that he makes the bold statement, "Every successful person defines their goals in writing." Research shows that less than 10% of the population actually put their goals in writing, but of those who do, 85% achieve them.

Developing goals is predominantly a matter of structure and organization. A poster on the wall of a gym states, "A goal is a dream with a deadline." You might alternately say "A goal without a timeline is just a dream."

It may be helpful to use "the three V's" in planning your goals:

> *Values—determine your core values, then determine your goals*
> *Vision—give your goals a vision*
> *Voice—give your goals a voice*

The difference between goals and a vision is that goals are activities you want to accomplish and a vision is what motivates you to set those goals. That is why determining your mission statements, as we did in the previous chapter, was a vital step in the goal-setting process.

Richard Suinn, Ph.D., is a sports psychologist and was the first to serve on a U.S. Olympic sports medicine team. He states:

> "Instead of just getting athletes 'psyched up,' we prefer to help them become more definite about why they're doing what they're doing now, even though their eventual goal—say winning a gold medal—may be a few years down the road. Goal setting helps to bring the future a little closer by breaking it down into steps to take this week, next week, and next month. That way, athletes can chart their progress, keeping in mind

where they're eventually going to end up. It enables those who are feeling that they want to give up to stay with the program (1999)."

In setting goals, it is helpful to construct meaning around the goal. Oprah Winfrey says, "As much as my work in television has been a big dream, the truth is that I never set out to create this huge life…the path to success was never about attaining incredible wealth or celebrity. It was about the process of continually seeking to be better, to challenge myself to pursue excellence on every level (May, 2002)." So, ask yourself, "What is my path to success about? How will the attainment of this goal change my life? How will it make my life *better*?"

Goals need to have three elements. They need a noun, a verb, and a deadline. The simplest goal statement I can think of is "Do it now."

—When you want something you've never had, you've got to do something you've never done.

—Unknown

10 Ways to Make Action = Results

1) Start with the end in mind.

2) Develop a clear and easy picture of what you want to accomplish. President Kennedy's goal "to send a man to the moon and bring him safely back home within this decade," was simple, but definite.

3) Write it down—COMMIT!

4) Break the job into measurable steps with completion dates.

5) Enlist the support of others—go public with your goals.

6) Get a coach. Even friends and/or family can serve as advisors to report progress to.

7) Enlist a team to help each other reach goals. An example of this would be a book writing group. You may each be working on a different book, but the others can assist you on format, etc…and vice versa.

8) Keep allies on your side and enemies at bay.

9) Celebrate progress—reward yourself.

10)   Thank those who have helped you along the way.

—I look beyond where others have been to see where I would go.
                                                        —Paul Conrad

The Only Way to Handle "Overwhelm"

Often, people are unable to begin pursuing a goal because they have too many goals, not all of which can be undertaken at once. If you prioritize your goals, you can then tackle the more important ones first. Undertaking these goals one at a time is the ONLY way to handle the overwhelm that the mass of them together present. Less critical or less immediate goals can be pursued later. Completing the time line exercise that follows is one way of remembering and committing to later goals while still pursuing only a limited number at the present time.

If you are having difficulty prioritizing, refer back to the "values based decision making" technique mentioned in Chapter Two. Many times people have difficulty differentiating between their WANTS and their SHOULDS. If your priorities are all based on SHOULDS, you may find that you do not feel very passionate or enthusiastic about your life or your goals. *Desire* is what creates energy and enthusiasm.

It is important to continue to monitor your goals and modify them when necessary. Desires change over time. You should realize that it is okay to modify your goals from time to time, however, if you are changing your mind constantly, you will never fully achieve anything of value.

—He who would learn to fly one day must first learn to stand and walk and run and climb and dance; one cannot fly into flying.
—Friedrich Nietzsche

Create Your Road Map that Gets You Where You Want to Go

Sub-goals strengthen motivation because they make an activity manageable and accessible. When a larger goal is divided into sub-goals, it becomes a series of incremental tasks rather than one overwhelming project. This idea has been expressed in many slogans that you can repeat to yourself to increase and sustain the motivation to stick with your goals:

- *By the inch it's a cinch, by the yard it's hard.*
- *One day at a time (From Alcoholics Anonymous).*
- *Just put one foot in front of the other.*
- *Baby steps.*
- *Nothin' to it but to do it!*

Sometimes, it is more profitable to block out the daunting, long-range picture of your goals in order to focus more completely on the immediate step that needs to be undertaken.

—Constantly ask yourself, "How is this action moving me toward my goals?"
—Lyn Kelley

Your Own Reward

To remain on your path toward goal achievement, it is important to measure your progress. When you complete sub-goals and tasks, you can cross them off your plan. When they are completed according to your time line, you may want to draw a happy face next to them (or some other symbol that makes you smile), as encouragement. It is important for your motivation to measure the amount of work accomplished and mark its place on the plan, as this demonstrates that there is progress being made. Task completion creates feelings of positive self-esteem. Goal achievement leads to feelings of self-confidence. Success breeds success. When you feel that you have mastered a project, you will be more motivated to start the next one.

Research has shown that subjects utilizing a "reward" system have better results. Rewards can be internal, such as feeling good about yourself, or they can be external, such as spending the day doing something fun. Something as small as "positive self statements" as self reward, may even be sufficient. Keeping a journal of steps and sub-goals that have been met is a tangible way to measure progress and feel good about it. Try coming up with your own ideas to incorporate healthy rewards for yourself as you accomplish your goals.

—You have to leave the city of your comfort and go into the wilderness of your intention. What you'll discover will be yourself.
—Alan Alda

Exercise 5:1
Creating an Action Plan

In his book, *Simple Steps to Impossible Dreams*, Steven Scott (1998) refers to the process of achieving your "dream" as the "Dream Conversion Process." He divides it into the following steps:

1) Define your dream in writing;
2) Convert your dream into specific goals;
3) Convert each goal into specific steps;
4) Convert each step into specific tasks;
5) Assign a projected time or date to complete each task.

We all have dreams and desires for our future. I would like you to take a moment to work through your own "Dream Conversion Process".

1) First, choose a dream that seems on the surface to be impossible to reach.

2) Next, determine what specific goals that dream is comprised of.

3) Write down from one to three goal statements that will make your dream a reality (make sure they include a noun, verb, and deadline).

4) Now, break those individual goals down into even smaller steps.

5) Once you have the steps in place, write down what it will take to reach that first step.

6) And finally, assign a projected time of completion for each of these tasks.

—Nothing happens until something moves.

—Albert Einstein

Exercise 5:2
Time Line

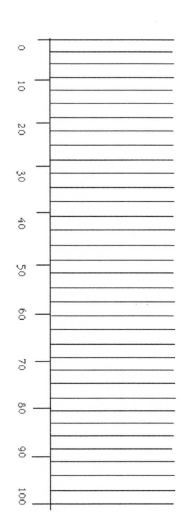

The time line drawn below corresponds to your life. Write down at the appropriate points your past accomplishments and future goals. Often, looking at the larger picture makes it easier to give up certain things for the moment and focus on others. You are not necessarily giving things up, but merely postponing them. When you are caught up in the middle of the struggle, take a moment to look at this time line and reflect on all that you have accomplished and all the time left for accomplishing future goals.

Exercise 5:3
Creating My Action Plan: Setting Goals, Sub-goals, Tasks Practice Goal planning Sheet

Refer back to the eight areas for which you developed mission statements. Then create a "goal statement" for each mission statement on each of the following eight pages. An example of a goal statement is "I will increase my exercise routine from 3 to 4 days a week by the end of this month." Remember, a goal without a *timeline* is just a "wish." Now, you will develop an action plan for each of those areas. Each goal statement usually involves sub goals in order to make the main goal happen. For example, in order to increase my exercise routine, I may have to ask my boss for one afternoon a week off work, cut my grocery shopping down to one day a week, and arrange child care for one extra day a week.

Each sub goal requires one or more tasks. Each task may even require several sub tasks that need to be done before that task can be accomplished. Each goal is made up of a series of action steps. If you look at everything that needs to be done it can seem overwhelming. However, once the tasks are outlined, you can just look at one task at a time. Remember, "By the inch it's a cinch, by the hard it's hard."

> *—The road to success is always under construction.*
>
> —Lily Tomlin

1. <u>Physical/Emotional Health:</u>

Goal statement : _____

_____

_____

Specific Steps:	Specific Tasks	Completion Date:
1. _____	_____	_____
	_____	_____
	_____	_____
2. _____	_____	_____
	_____	_____
	_____	_____
3. _____	_____	_____
	_____	_____
	_____	_____
4. _____	_____	_____
	_____	_____
	_____	_____

2. Relationship/Marriage:

Goal statement : _____

_____

_____

Specific Steps:	Specific Tasks	Completion Date:
1. _____	_____	_____
	_____	_____
	_____	_____
	_____	_____
2. _____	_____	_____
	_____	_____
	_____	_____
	_____	_____
3. _____	_____	_____
	_____	_____
	_____	_____
	_____	_____
4. _____	_____	_____
	_____	_____
	_____	_____
	_____	_____

3. <u>Family:</u>

Goal statement : _____

_____

_____

Specific Steps:	Specific Tasks	Completion Date:
1. _____	_____	_____
	_____	_____
	_____	_____
2. _____	_____	_____
	_____	_____
	_____	_____
3. _____	_____	_____
	_____	_____
	_____	_____
4. _____	_____	_____
	_____	_____
	_____	_____
	_____	_____

4. Professional/Career:

Goal statement : _____
_____
_____

Specific Steps:	Specific Tasks	Completion Date:
1. _____	_____	_____
	_____	_____
	_____	_____
2. _____	_____	_____
	_____	_____
	_____	_____
3. _____	_____	_____
	_____	_____
	_____	_____
4. _____	_____	_____
	_____	_____
	_____	_____
	_____	_____

5. <u>Financial:</u>

Goal statement : _____

_____

_____

Specific Steps:	Specific Tasks	Completion Date:
1. _____	_____	_____
	_____	_____
	_____	_____
	_____	_____
2. _____	_____	_____
	_____	_____
	_____	_____
	_____	_____
3. _____	_____	_____
	_____	_____
	_____	_____
	_____	_____
4. _____	_____	_____
	_____	_____
	_____	_____
	_____	_____

6. Social/Political:

Goal statement : _____

_____

_____

Specific Steps:	Specific Tasks	Completion Date:
1. _____	_____	_____
	_____	_____
	_____	_____
2. _____	_____	_____
	_____	_____
	_____	_____
3. _____	_____	_____
	_____	_____
	_____	_____
4. _____	_____	_____
	_____	_____
	_____	_____
	_____	_____

7. <u>Spiritual:</u>

Goal statement : _____

_____

_____

Specific Steps: Specific Tasks   Completion Date:

1. _____   _____   _____

                    _____   _____

                    _____   _____

2. _____   _____   _____

                    _____   _____

                    _____   _____

3. _____   _____   _____

                    _____   _____

                    _____   _____

4. _____   _____   _____

                    _____   _____

                    _____   _____

8. Hobbies/Recreation:

Goal statement : _____

_____

_____

Specific Steps:	Specific Tasks	Completion Date:
1. _____	_____	_____
	_____	_____
	_____	_____
	_____	_____
2. _____	_____	_____
	_____	_____
	_____	_____
	_____	_____
3. _____	_____	_____
	_____	_____
	_____	_____
	_____	_____
4. _____	_____	_____
	_____	_____
	_____	_____
	_____	_____

—A goal without an action plan is a daydream.
                              —Dr. Nathaniel Brandon

Chapter Six:
Get Out of Your Own Way!

The Three Brutal Mistakes that Cause Your Self-Sabotage

The next seven chapters were easy for me to write because I have done all seven self sabotages (some of them many times over). I have sabotaged my success in so many ways that I would be ashamed to list them. I've gotten in my own way in my relationships, my career, my education, my health, my finances and my sanity and peace of mind. I've delayed my success far longer than I should have. I've wasted time on things that were clearly not in my best interest. I've gone through tremendous pain at times when I didn't need to.

The three brutal mistakes people make that cause their own sabotage are:

1. Staying in their comfort zone
2. Inability to predict and manage risk
3. Denying the part of themselves that wants to create, grow and improve

Beware. In your pursuit of success, you will find that you will encounter many fears, obstacles and hardships that will take you outside your comfort zone. There will be a strong pull to stop your efforts. You will be tempted to return to your comfort zone. This is normal. There may be times when you will need to stop for a while, in order to adjust to the changes you are encountering. Sometimes it takes time to adjust to a new level of "havingness." Your psyche needs to adjust to the changes. Even positive change is stressful. Allow yourself some time to relax, then "psyche yourself up" to move on to the next task in your pursuit.

There are also times when we are so uncomfortable with change, that we will actually sabotage our own success. We are uncomfortable because things are not familiar. The subconscious mind equates "familiar" with "safe." Therefore, anything that does not feel familiar may feel unsafe, thereby causing a great deal of anxiety. Our anxiety may manifest itself in mild to serious sabotage. Some people are afraid of failure, while others are afraid of success. This is what keeps us stuck in the status quo, conforming to the "norm" as we see it. You need to evaluate your risk—whether it is too risky or too comfortable. This evaluation is an ongoing internal and external process.

As I write this book I am plagued with "writer's block." This is the inability to act on what I say I want to do. I often hear people say "I want to do it but I just can't seem to get myself to do it." When this happens, the person is in touch with their "wanting to" but not in touch with their "not-wanting to" which is preventing their action. Action blocks are usually forms of denial or "dissociation." It is important to get in touch with the part of you that wants to change, grow, create and improve.

It is also very helpful to get some therapy or coaching at this point, as many of these exercises will bring up issues you may need assistance in working through. A good coach or therapist can also help you create a "genogram" which is a family map. Find out what success level your relatives achieved and what may have blocked them from further success. This can help you to either re-create some of their positive achievements and to not repeat their blocks. The following seven chapters are the seven main patterns of success blockers and ways to overcome each.

> — *...and then the day came when the risk to remain tight in a bud was more painful than the risk it took to blossom.*
>
> —Anais Nin

Let's Get Off Our "But's"

As I mentioned earlier, if you are not already taking action toward your goal, it is either not what you *really* want or you have obstacles that need to be overcome. Let's take Donna for example. Donna states she would like to be a competitive tennis player. Donna has been thinking about playing tennis for quite some time, but has not yet started playing. She has not even started reading about tennis or watching tennis matches. Not only has she never played tennis, she hasn't even found out where the tennis courts are in her neighborhood. She does not own a tennis racquet and has not signed up for lessons. My question to Donna would be, "Is playing tennis competitively what you really, really, really, really want? Or is it just a wish or fantasy?" If she says it is what she really wants, then I would ask her, "Why haven't you started yet?" I would find out what her obstacles are (or her perceived obstacles) and determine if this goal is realistic for her, or if it is her true desire. If it is a strong desire, I would recommend coaching for her to assist her in overcoming her obstacles so she can begin taking action.

You see, if you *really, really, really, really* want something, you will start right away! Your passion for this desire will be so strong that you won't be able to NOT do it! You will at least be taking action steps toward your goal. After you have completed the next seven chapters, you should either begin taking action toward your goal, or seriously reconsider your goal.

—People are always blaming their circumstances for where they are. I don't believe in circumstances. The people who get on in this world are the people who get up and look for the circumstances they want, and if they can't find them, make them.

—George Bernard Shaw

Exercise 6:1
Self-Sabotages

For each of the following, list at least one way you have sabotaged your own success in the past. Then write an affirmation about how you will not sabotage yourself this way ever again.

Love Relationships:

Friendships:

Family Relationships:

Physical Health/Appearance:

Emotional/Mental Health:

Spiritual Health/Peace:

Career:

Finances:

Education/Learning:

Productivity/Creativity:

Hobbies/Recreation:

Other:

—No one can go back and make a brand new start, but anyone can start from now and make a brand new ending.
                                                                    —Unknown

Part II:

THE SEVEN SELF-SABOTAGES TO YOUR SUCCESS

Chapter Seven:
Self Sabotage #1:
"It's Just Too Difficult"

Why Action is So Hard

Even after you have created a vision statement and action plan, one of the greatest roadblocks to success remains the lack of sustained, concerted effort. Most people are somewhat lazy; our natural tendency is to avoid stress and dedication (however, I know this doesn't apply to *you*). Most of us prefer to do what is fun, easy, and immediate. As previously mentioned, we are constantly pulled back to our "comfort zone."

As an example, the American Dietary Association completed a survey in which they reported that two-thirds of American adults do not eat a nutritious diet. The three main reasons people gave for not eating nutritiously were:

1) They do not want to give up taste
2) They do not want to take the extra time
3) It's too difficult in general

When considering your goals and action plan, it is also critical to remember to create goals that are realistic, healthy and attainable. In the previous chapter we discussed how to choose your goals, how to assess the healthiness of your goals, and how to have "optimally challenging" goals, those that are not too difficult and not too easy. It is important to note that most of us, particularly women, *tend to reach too **low** rather than too high*. Obviously, reaching too high can lead to chronic self defeat. However, reaching too *low* can lead to chronic underachieving. Underachievers always seem to feel unsettled because there is a part of them that "knows" they are not living up to their potential. They tend to make life choices far beneath their capabilities, desires and dreams. They often "settle" when it comes to choosing mates, friends, co-workers, etc…This "settling" is a major self sabotage, causing problems and setbacks with long term ramifications. Take a minute to contemplate this. Are you typically happy with the choices you make in life, or do you find you tend to reach too low or too high?

You may also become frustrated by thinking, "This is just taking *too long*." This is probably the number one reason people do not stick with their goals. By nature we want instant gratification, particularly in the Western culture. *We want what we want and we want it NOW!* Often, the payoff simply does not coming quickly enough to satisfy us. The fact is that most things of value in life do take time to achieve.

—Make stepping stones out of stumbling blocks.

—Unknown

How to "Just Do It"

You will find that changing self statements from negative to positive can be very beneficial during this struggle. Try to look at the change process as a long road or journey. Describe the path you are on, and where it leads. Describe where you are tempted to veer off, and where that "veered off" path is likely to take you. Remind yourself of the value of staying true to your path, if in fact, your desired success is somewhere along it, even if it takes a long time. Just know that you don't have to *want* to do it, or *feel* like doing it—just DO it! The saying "When the going gets tough, the tough get going," describes the inner strength you may need to summons in order to continue. It takes tremendous courage, determination and tenacity to continue, or get back up after a fall, during rough times. Support, validation and encouragement from others are especially important here.

The most difficult thing to do is to discipline ourselves to focus and concentrate, especially when a more immediately gratifying activity beckons. As I write this book, I am thinking about how nice it would be to be lying on the beach reading a good book. However, I write instead because I keep the vision of my reward foremost in my mind.

The best way to "just do it" is to keep your vision of your desired result in front of you. Keep pictures of your vision everywhere you can see them. Keep telling yourself and others that you will reach your goal. For example, "I will start college in September of 2008, and I will finish in June of 2012, and I will land my fabulous job within two months of graduation."

—Great works are performed not by strength, but by perseverance.
                                                    —Samuel Johnson

Exercise 7:1
Review Your Past Successes

List 10 successes that you have achieved. In the box provided after each one, describe what motivated you to achieve the goal, the obstacles you overcame to achieve it, and how you felt when you succeeded:

My Successes	Motivation	Obstacles	Feeling after Completion

Chapter Eight:
Self-Sabotage #2:
"I Don't Deserve It"

Pump Up Your Self Worth

"I don't deserve it" is often an underlying, unconscious thought. It has a great deal to do with one's self-esteem, feelings of competency and self worth. Self-esteem is an extremely important part of achieving your goals. You can only pursue and keep what you think you deserve. Consequently, lack of self-esteem will sabotage your attempts at success. When you lack self-esteem, an internalized critical inner voice will attempt to cancel your ambitions through self-doubt and disbelief. In *Taming the Inner Critic* (1997), Ernest Isaacs argues that if your "inner critic" is brought to your attention, then this critical voice can be consciously rebuffed and refuted. With this insight, you can arm yourself with ammunition to stop the process of self-sabotage.

Positive affirmations can replace former negative ones. Avoid making statements to yourself such as, "My father was right, I'll never succeed at anything." When a statement like that comes into your head, try to dispel it by immediately reminding yourself of something you have recently succeeded at. Wayne Dyer, the popular self-help author, says that by working through self-defeating labels and behaviors, people can build confidence and self-esteem so that there are no limits to what they can achieve. Come up with your own positive statements about yourself. A negative statement should be immediately replaced with a positive one. Another technique for changing negative self-talk to positive is known as "Stop-Think." As soon as a negative thought comes into your head, immediately think "STOP!" and change over to a positive thought that has been prepared to replace the negative one.

—Our deepest fear is not that we are inadequate. Our deepest fear is that we are powerful beyond measure. It is our light, not our darkness, that most frightens us. We ask ourselves, 'Who am I to be brilliant, gorgeous, talented and fabulous?' Actually, who are you NOT to be? You are a child of God. Your 'playing small' does not serve the world. There is nothing enlightened about shrinking so that other people don't feel insecure around you. We were born to make manifest the glory of God that is within us. It's not just in some of us. It's in everyone. And as you let your light shine, you unconsciously give other people permission to do the same. As you are liberated from your own fears, your presence automatically liberates others.

—Nelson Mandela

Shame and Guilt—The Ultimate Destroyers

Another possible problem is unconscious *guilt* about your own success or "havingness." Many people describe a feeling of shame, or "awaiting punishment" when their lives are going well. Often, we hear things like, "Things are going *too* well. I'm just looking over my shoulder waiting for something bad to happen." It is as if every good thing must be followed by a bad thing. People talk about going through a "lucky streak" followed by a "streak of bad luck." These kinds of statements need to be recognized as self-sabotage. They should be replaced with positive statements and affirmations. The world is not out to get you!

Wayne Dyer, in his book *The Sky's the Limit* (1980) does an excellent job of dealing with unhealthy guilt. He discusses the "guilt myth," wherein a person might believe "If I'm prospering, other people may be starving." The truth is, he explains, that the more you prosper, the better position you are in to help others in need. People will starve whether or not you prosper—your "having more" does not take something away from someone else (unless of course, you've stolen it!). In fact, Dyer states, you can create better lives for others when you improve your own life. When you earn more money you either save it or spend it, and pay taxes on it. Any way you use your money you are helping the national (and global) economy.

—The maxim "Nothing avails but perfection" may be spelled "Paralysis."
—Sir Winston Churchill

Talk Back to Your Inner Critic

If you feel shame and guilt you probably have a very strong tendency to "parent" yourself. Freud described the three parts of our mind as the "id" (child), the "ego" (adult) and the "superego" (parent). A mentally healthy person relies mostly on his/her "adult" to modify his/her "child" and "parent." It is the "parent" part of us that is the "judge" and "critic." We tend to be far worse punishers of ourselves than anyone else has ever been.

Our "inner critic" says things to us like "You stupid idiot! How could you have said/done something like that? You screwed it all up and everything is ruined and it's all your fault!" Each time this happens our self esteem goes down a notch and we feel less adequate and more inferior. At these times it is up to our "adult" to step in and give some reality to our situation. For example, our "adult" might respond to our "parent" by saying "You know, it was just a mistake. Everyone makes mistakes sometimes. Not everything is ruined, it's just a setback." You can take responsibility by owning up to your mistake, apologizing if appropriate, accepting the consequences with dignity, then move on.

A helpful exercise is called "the empty chair." Sit in a chair and place an empty chair in front of you. Imagine this empty chair is your "parent" and you are your "adult." Talk to "the parent" and tell it that while it is sometimes helpful to keep you in line, this time it has gone too far. Let your parent know the limits you will accept. Let your parent know it is not okay to be harshly critical and judgmental. It is not okay to make you feel worthless. It is not okay to "catastrophize" the situation by making it out to be much worse than it really is. It is not okay to "should all over you."

The "parent's" place is to keep us from going too far in any direction, remind us of right and wrong, and keep us safe. It is to support, guide and encourage us. It is not to condemn us, make us wrong, inadequate, insecure, afraid, incompetent or inferior. Sometimes I have to get really mad at my "parent" and yell at it! I've been known to yell at my empty chair, "I will not allow you to shame me. I will not allow you to cause me to be depressed or fearful! How dare you rob me of my self worth! How dare you rob me of my happiness and joy! Back off and do your job of supporting, validating and encouraging!" I always feel a lot better afterward!

—You will succeed best when you put the restless, anxious side of affairs out of mind, and allow the restful side to live in your thoughts.
—Margaret Stowe

Turn "Learned Helplessness" into "Learned Empowerment"

Martin Seligman, past president of the American Psychological Association wrote a book called *Learned Helplessness* (1990). Learned helplessness is the theory that one develops feelings of helplessness when one feels that the consequences of his/her behavior occur independently of their action and are thus beyond their control. In other words, the reason I did well in this swim meet was because the top two swimmers were ill, or the reason I did poorly on this test was because the teacher only asked questions that weren't on the study guide. Therefore, we do not take any personal responsibility (credit or blame) for what happens to us. This is a major hindrance to one's motivation.

People who are in a state of "learned helplessness" often see themselves as victims. They see someone or something else controlling them, and feel helpless to stop it. An example would be a woman who discovers an ex-boyfriend is stalking her, yet she continues to talk with him on the phone. She gives her stalker "hope" rather than demanding he stop his behavior and/or get help from others to make it stop and get protection for herself.

When you notice a feeling of helplessness or powerlessness in a particular area, you should practice new self-statements regarding your personal strength and confidence. An example of a new pro-active self-statement would be, "It is my *decisions*, not my *conditions*, that determine my destiny."

—If you think you're too small to make a difference, you haven't been in bed with a mosquito.

—Unknown

Exercise 8:1
Your 10 Signature Strengths

One way to overcome "learned helplessness" is to identify your 5 greatest strengths and stop obsessing over your weaknesses. Signature strengths are the positive traits you feel have brought you the most success and happiness in life. They are qualities you possess that you are proud of, and that others have complimented you on.

Examples of signature strengths are; 1) I'm generous, 2) My life is balanced and functional, 3) I'm debt-free, 4) I'm a caring, loving friend and relative, 5) I'm a high achiever, 6) I'm determined to get what I want, 7) I'm powerful and influential, 8) I care about others and they know it, 9) I'm a good mother, and 10) I keep my word.

If you are not sure of your greatest strengths, ask several trusted people in your life to tell you what they think they are. You'll be amazed at what they say!

1. Brainstorm all your positive qualities below:

2. List your 10 signature (greatest) strengths:

—It takes time to succeed because success is merely the natural reward for taking time to do anything well.

—Joseph Ross

Chapter Nine:
Self-Sabotage #3:
"I Don't Have the Time"

It's Not About Time—It's About Goal Conflict

Time. There is only so much time in a day, and only so much time in a lifetime. One of the most widespread problems in dealing with the "time" issue is *goal conflict.* This means having multiple, conflicting goals, such as a teenager's desire for both total independence and a safe, nurturing home environment. Another example would be the adult who wants career success but wants to avoid having to work extra hours. These conflicts tend to lead to inaction, since the pursuit of one goal entails the betrayal of another goal. It is important to first clarify your values and then prioritize your goals accordingly.

In Chapter Two I discussed values clarification. Refer back to *Exercises 2:1 and 2:2,* in which you made an assessment of your personal values. Now, determine which goal is more in line with your true values. Once you have done that, look at what you really want. Draw up a list of the pros and cons of possible paths and then come up with the best action to take at the current time.

> —*To be what we are, and to become what we are capable of becoming is the only end of life.*
>
> —Robert Louis Stevenson

Work Smarter—Not Harder or Longer

Sometimes goals are not inherently contradictory, and in this case you can simply concentrate on achieving one goal at a time. If the goals are concurrent ones, such as being a top employee of a law firm, spending time with one's children, and becoming an expert rock-climber, you can often delegate aspects of these various goals: Perhaps some of your duties at work can be delegated. Even if this means a slight cut in pay, it might be worth it if it allows you to continue a job while simultaneously being a good parent and pursuing an interest in rock climbing. As you can see, values clarification is a vitally important step towards reaching your goals. It may seem initially that taking a possible cut in pay is not a logical option, but if you value the time off to pursue your rock climbing interest and you can live more or less comfortably on less money, it may be worth it to you—only *you* can make that determination.

Finding time to work on your goals (or anything else for that matter) is simply a matter of organization and planning. You can "work smarter" by spending 15 to 30 minutes in the morning to plan your day. You will need to discipline yourself to stick to your plan. Allow time in between for interruptions that may be necessary to deal with, but do the best you can at sticking to your plan. I make a list of all the things I want to accomplish each day, then I cross each item off my list as it is completed. Because I was a single, working mother, getting my Ph.D. took me five years. I put one half hour a day into my program and in five years I was finished!

—Anything worth doing is worth doing badly, until you get it right.
—Les Brown

See the Bigger Picture

Goal conflict can also serve as an excuse for abandoning goals before they are complete. Exercises such as time management and creating a "life time line" can be very helpful (see Exercise 5:2). Also, remember that you can do almost *anything* you want, but you cannot do *everything* you want, and certainly not all at the same time! You will need to prioritize and take things one at a time.

Think of your life as a bigger picture. While most people live to 80 years old now, it is predicted that soon most of us will live to 100 or more. There are many, many successful people who achieved great things after 90 years of age! Next time the thought, "I wish I had…but I'm too old now," comes into your head, just remember that age is not a deterrent as evidenced by many people who accomplished amazing things later in life. Add to this list some role models of your own.

- At 99, David Eugene Ray of Tennessee learned to read.
- At 91, Hulda Crooks climbed Mount Whitney, the highest mountain in the continental U.S.
- At 97, Martin Miller of Indiana was working full time as a lobbyist for older citizens.
- At age 51, when most people are planning their retirements, Ray Crock made his first hamburger. He grew this one stand into the world's largest food chain.
- At 99, the twin sisters Kin Narita and Gin Kanie recorded a hit single in Japan and starred in a TV commercial.
- At 96, Kathrine Robinson Everett was practicing law in North Carolina.
- At 95, the choreographer Martha Graham prepared her modern dance troupe for its latest performance.
- At 94, George Burns performed at Proctor's Theater in Schenectady, NY—63 years after he first played there.
- At 93, Dame Judith Anderson, the actress, gave a one–hour benefit performance.
- At 92, Paul Spangler completed his 14th marathon.

> *—You have powers you never dreamed of. You can do things you never thought you could do. There are no limitations in what you can do except the limitations of your own mind.*
> —Darwin P. Kingsley

The Simple Reason Why Change is So Hard

There is an old saying, "The only guarantees in life are change, death and taxes." The book *Who Moved My Cheese?* (2000) is about mice who's cheese has been moved to a new place in their maze. How the different mice go about finding their cheese demonstrates healthy vs. unhealthy coping styles. As we hurdle along at breakneck speed, we are now caught up in the most rapidly changing society in the history of mankind. We need to be able to cope with the changes—better yet—foresee the changes—and prepare for them before they come. While change can be frustrating, staying up with the changes is rewarding because, as the book says, "Having cheese makes you happy."

What is your cheese? It may be more money, a new car, a new house, more time with your family, more time for your hobbies, more peace and balance, a college education for your kids, etc. Whatever your cheese is, I want you to have it.

The simple reason why change is so hard is because we resist it. The definition of homeostasis is: That which works to keep things the same, even when things aren't very good. We are creatures of habit, and prefer to stay in our routines. We are more comfortable when in our "comfort zone." The only way to make your life better is to accept that it will require change and allow the change to come. You can choose to flow through the changes rather than fight them.

Sometimes life throws changes at us, and we are forced off course for a while. Setbacks and delays are to be expected and accepted as a part of life. There may be times when you simply do not have the energy, stamina, or motivation to continue on your path. Some days you just won't feel like exercising. Some days you just won't feel like dieting. Some days you just won't feel like studying, working, writing, whatever it is. Take care of yourself by giving yourself permission for some time off. You may even use "time off" as a reward for accomplishing an especially difficult task. You need to trust your instincts, and when your instincts are telling you it's too much right now, then take a rest. This poem exemplifies this point.

Keeping Still
Keeping Still means stopping.
When it is time to stop, then stop.
When it is time to advance, then advance.
Thus movement and rest
Do not miss the right time.
And their course becomes
Bright and clear.

—*I Ching, Hexagram 52, Sixth Century B.C.*

Exercise 9:1
Time Management Pie

Think about the way you usually spend your time: the amount of time you allot to sleep, to work, to exercise, to spending time with family and friends, to watching TV, etc. Cut the <u>first</u> pie into pieces representing amounts of time you spend *currently* on each activity. Then cut the <u>second</u> pie into pieces representing the amounts of time *you would like* to spend on each activity.

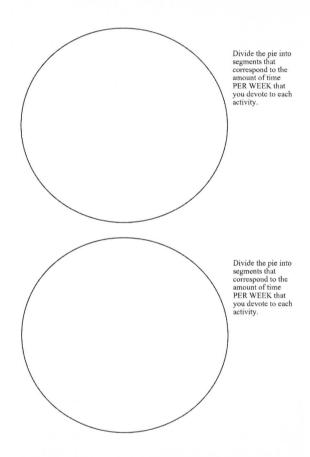

Divide the pie into segments that correspond to the amount of time PER WEEK that you devote to each activity.

Divide the pie into segments that correspond to the amount of time PER WEEK that you devote to each activity.

—The secret of getting ahead is getting started. The secret of getting started is breaking your complex overwhelming tasks into small manageable tasks, and then starting on the first one.

—Mark Twain

Chapter Ten:
Self Sabotage #4:
"I Don't Have the Resources"

Nice But Not Necessary

Tony Robbins says, "More than anything else, I believe it's our *decisions*, not the *conditions* of our lives that determine our destiny." Most of us can give lots of excuses as to why we cannot achieve our true goals. Most of these excuses center on not having certain resources or advantages. Having resources is nice, but not necessary. We all know of people who had tremendous opportunity and resources to do whatever they wanted in life and chose not to take advantage of it. We also know of people who had very little opportunity and resources yet ended up achieving great things.

It is true that some people do have unfair advantages; be they genetic, educational, environmental, monetary, or familial. But in *Simple Steps to Impossible Dreams*, Steven Scott (1998) insists that people who achieve "impossible dreams" are generally not very different in resources from the average person:

> They _don't_ have higher IQs;
> They have _not_ been better educated;
> They do _not_ have better backgrounds than you do.

> They simply learned and utilized some specific techniques that enabled them to 'dream big' and then to achieve those dreams.

When you find yourself thinking about how others were blessed with advantages and you were not, remind yourself about the many people who, by making decisions about their lives and pursuing their goals, overcame the odds and achieved extraordinary success that far exceeded their conditions. *Biography Magazine* is filled with examples of people who have done great things with few resources and poor conditions.

—Success leaves clues.

—Anthony Robbins

How Role Models and Mentors Zoom You to the Top

Another great strategy is to go to a library or bookstore and research people who have succeeded at goals similar to your own. Read biographies, watch movies, listen to audio tapes, etc. Take notes on obstacles that they successfully overcame and on their strategies for achieving their goals. There are countless biographies and stories on famous and not so famous people who have achieved great things with very little.

A famous line from a poem states, "I grew taller today from walking through the trees." In the same way, we can become like our role models just by learning about them, watching them, studying them, and listening to them. We can put ourselves in their shoes, so to speak, and try out what it would be like to walk in them. This also helps us to "de-pedastalize" them. We often put certain people up on a pedestal, thinking they are way above us, beyond our reach, super human—in another world. The reality is, they are just human beings like us. If you are interested in people for whom faith and belief were integral to success, a useful book to consider is *One Who Believed: True Stories of Faith*, by Robert B. Pamplin (1993).

Hearing the personal histories of people who overcame hardship and proved wrong those who had given up on them can be an inspiring experience for many. The reason this strategy works so well is that people learn from imitation. It is helpful to have a model of a person (or several people) with whom one can identify—someone who has had similar struggles and has overcome them. One is thus led to think, if so-and-so could do it, why can't I? The stories have the effect of making one identify with a community of survivors, of confident people who believed in themselves and achieved success because of their determination.

Personally, I have made a point to go see and hear at least one person each quarter who is doing what I want to be doing. I want to share their space. I want to share molecules with them. This way I feel I'm getting to know them on a more personal level. Seeing, hearing, and touching my mentors causes me to feel more connected to them, and decreases the imagined "distance" between us. It makes me realize that I am not very different from them.

When I visit my mentors I ask myself, "What kind of person would he/she have to be in order to do what he/she is doing?" I write down those attributes and ask myself if I could be that kind of person. If I feel I could, I try to step into their shoes.

> —*Spock had a huge effect on me. Playing the character so often actually made me more rational and logical.*
>
> —Leonard Nemoy

Extraordinary People Who Have Done More With Less

Here are some examples to get you started. If you are intrigued by these anecdotes, you can do further research on the people whose lives and successes they
recount:

* Motivational author and speaker Tony Robbins contends that his own
rags-to-riches story proves that success "requires internal commitment, not
external credentials." Robbins, who earns up to $60,000 a day conducting cor-
porate seminars and $12 million or more a year selling motivational books and
tapes, is a high school graduate with no formal training, no professional
license, and no academic degree. For Robbins, confidence and determination
are the crucial elements that enable success.

* Albert Einstein was born with a misshapen head and an abnormally large
body. He learned to talk so late that his parents feared he was mentally
retarded. He was also so withdrawn that one governess named him "Father
Bore." Because he found schoolwork (especially memorization) tedious, he
paid little attention. As a result, many of his teachers dismissed him as dimwit-
ted. He dropped out of high school and failed a technical college entrance
exam. When his interest was piqued by a home tutor, however, he proved to be
a genius. His calling just happened to be higher mathematics. No one is successful at everything. A critical component of motivation and success is finding one's niche, one's gifts, one's passion.

* Michael Jordan, one of the best basketball players of all time, amazed us
by breaking his own personal records over and over. He has said that what
motivates him is the challenge. When Jordan hears a sportscaster (or a com-
petitor), express doubts that he can rise to the occasion, or state that his team
is not favored to win, he simply hears it as a challenge, which serves to
increase his motivation to prove himself capable and to prove his challengers
wrong. You may have encountered similar criticism from others: someone in
your past told you that you couldn't do it. Someone may have told you that
you were a failure. You may have had negative labels placed on you by significant adults during your childhood. Jordan's determination exemplifies the
way in which these negative statements can be used as a positive motivational force, if they are viewed as a challenge rather than as confirmation of
unavoidable failure.

*J.K. Rowling, a divorced mom with a young daughter, scribbled Harry
Potter's story in Edinburgh cafes while getting by on public assistance. When
her first book was published in 1997, it was an almost instant success—and

from there, Rowling's fame and influence grew exponentially, her fortune now estimated at over $150 million. Her dream, she once said, was to "drive children back to reading books," and she has succeeded in magical fashion.

> —Nothing in the world will take the place of persistence. Talent will not, genius will not, education will not. Persistence and determination alone are omnipotent. Press on.
>
> —Calvin Coolidge

Exercise 10:1
I'm Confident I Can and Will Do It!

—Make sure you get your stars out.
—J.D. Salinger

What are Your Stars?

Fantasy Exercise: Imagine you are going to be honored for an achievement you made in your chosen field. You will be given an award of "Successful Achievement" at a national convention. The convention hosts will introduce you and speak about you prior to your acceptance of your award. Write their introduction and speech honoring you. Include all your prior accomplishments, training and experience. Write out all the qualities and attributes you would like them to mention. Write exactly what you did that you are being honored for. What are your stars? What would you like them to be? What would you like to be remembered for? Just for a few minutes, be as great as you can be!

—Those who are victorious plan effectively and change decisively. They are like a great river that maintains its course but adjusts its flow.
—Sun Tzu.

Chapter Eleven:
Self-Sabotage #5:
"I Have To Do It My Way"

Why Smart People Do Dumb Things

Why do smart/talented people sometimes do dumb things that cause them to self-destruct? Researchers have found some commonalities in people who have achieved a high level of success in a particular area of their lives, and who subsequently self-destructed or "crashed and burned"—failed school, got fired, got arrested, lost their families, went bankrupt, were impeached or otherwise fell from grace. It appears that the attitude of "having to do it my way" without regard for the impact on other people or allowing feedback or advice from others, often results in damaging consequences. Most of the problem seems to have to do with people who are over-determined to do things *their own way*. This can arise out of selfishness, rebellion, elitism, extreme self-reliance or a more deep seated emotional or psychological problem. Some experts believe that it has to do with the personal character of the person him/herself.

Some of the personal characteristics researchers have found that often lead to self-sabotage have to do with the following:

Self-centeredness
Arrogance
Denial
Isolation
Feeling "above reproach"
Impatience
Rebellion
Anger with aggression
Recklessness
Over-reaching
Over-risk taking
Impulsivity

Inability to ask for advice
Inability to ask for feedback
Inability to ask questions and listen
Lack of caring about others' feelings
Insistence on doing everything themselves
Stubbornness

"Sir, what is the secret of your success?" a reporter asked a bank president.
"Two words."
"And, sir, what are they?"
"Right decisions."
"And how do you make the right decisions?"
"One word."
"And, sir, what is it?"
"Experience."
"And how do you get experience?"
"Two words."
"And, sir, what are they?"
"Wrong decisions."

Why People Kick a Gift Horse in the Mouth

A common self sabotage for high achievers is "kicking a gift horse in the mouth." An example of this was displayed on an episode of the popular television reality show, *The Apprentice*. The prize for the Project Manager on the winning team would be exemption from being fired after the next task. One winning Project Manager decided to forfeit his "prize." The result was that he was on the losing team on the next task, was brought into the board room and subsequently fired. One of the main reasons Donald Trump gave for firing this person was that "he shot himself in the foot by giving away his prize."

Sometimes not being able to accept the "gifts and goodies" that are offered to us is a result of deep seated guilt, insecurity and unworthiness. It goes back to the feeling of "I don't deserve it." Other times this behavior is a result of arrogance and/or poor judgment. Sometimes it is a result of stubbornness and independence. Some people do not want anyone to "give" them anything; they want to do everything "on their own." They do not want to "owe" anyone anything, or share the credit for their "winnings" with anyone. Sometimes it is a matter of rebellion. People who repeatedly "kick a gift horse in the mouth" or "shoot themselves in the foot" are in a great deal of denial. They can benefit from getting assistance in confronting their deeper emotional issues. The frustrating thing is, many of these people are even too rebellious to ask for help.

—People seldom improve when they have no other model but themselves to copy.

—Oliver Goldsmith

How Addictions and Compulsions Destroy You

Another very common self sabotage among those who have risen to a high level of success is addictive/compulsive behaviors. It seems that high achievers and hard drivers have a high correlation to "taking a good thing too far." This often shows up as alcoholism, drug addiction, addictive gambling, extreme sports, etc. The definition of addiction is anything which you do that you cannot stop on your own. Addictions lead to failure and destruction.

If you feel addiction may be hindering your ability to achieve your goals, ask yourself these questions developed by John Knight, MD, Director of the Center for Adolescent Substance Abuse Research (and colleagues) at Children's Hospital in Boston, MA. You can change the words "alcohol and drugs" to whatever addiction may apply to you.

C.R.A.F.T.

C   Have you ever ridden in a CAR driven by someone (including yourself) who was "high" or had been using alcohol or drugs?

R   Do you ever use alcohol or drugs to RELAX, feel better about yourself, or fit in?

A   Do you ever use alcohol/drugs while you are by yourself, ALONE?

F   Do your relatives, friends or co-workers ever tell you that you should cut down on your drinking or drug use?

T   Have you gotten into TROUBLE while you were using alcohol or drugs?

If you answered "yes" to one or more of these questions, you may want to consider getting professional help as it will be very difficult to reach your full potential if addiction is present in your life.

—The great thing in life is not so much where we are, but in what direction we are moving.
> —Oliver Wendell Holmes

Exercise 11:1
Rate Your Ability to Remain Successful

Rate the following 1—4.

1 = Seldom   2 = Occasionally   3 = Often   4 = Frequently

1. ___I ask others what they think before I make a major change in my life/business.

2. ___I think before I speak about the effect my words may have on others.

3. ___I am aware of what I am feeling.

4. ___I am flexible and can modify my plans when needed.

5. ___I know my strengths and weaknesses.

6. ___I often get information and/or advice from others more knowledgeable or skilled than I am.

7. ___I deal calmly with stress.

8. ___I believe other people can usually be counted on to get the job done.

9. ___Others say I understand and am sensitive to them.

10. __Others say they feel they can be honest with me.

11. __I deal effectively with last minute change.

12. __I set measurable goals and complete tasks on time.

13. __I resolve conflicts with others rather quickly.

14. __I ask for feedback and evaluation from others about my work/skills.

—God gave us two ears but only one mouth. Some people say that's because He wanted us to spend twice as much time listening as talking. Others claim it's because He knew that listening was twice as hard.

—Anonymous

Chapter Twelve:
Self-Sabotage #6:
"They Don't Want Me To"

Validators vs. Invalidators

I cannot emphasize enough the power of role models, partners, mentors, sponsors, teachers and coaches. You need to surround yourself with a "team" of supporters. The word "team" represents a group of people who work together on one common goal. Your team is supporting *your* goal. Ask your teammates for support, validation and encouragement. If they aren't giving that to you, ask why.

The social context in which goals are pursued has a direct effect on motivation. Failure to handle this one aspect can sabotage all your best efforts! The presence of other people can either increase or decrease your desire to perform well. An example of how others can decrease motivation would be an employee who is constantly being watched and criticized by a boss while performing a task. This type of social feedback actually suppresses your ability to perform well, and will in fact cause you to err. Conversely, working on a project in a group with supportive people who all have the same goal and are depending upon each member of the group to do their part, can increase your ability to perform well.

BEWARE OF NEGATORS. The reason you don't need to put a lid on a bucket of live crabs is because they pull each other back down into the pot. There are two types of people to hang out with. Supporters or negators. Encouragers or suppressors. Validators or invalidators. Sometimes you don't have a choice, if this person is a family member who is living with you, or if they are a boss or co-worker. When you are around an invalidator and don't have a choice, you will need to at least confront it. Being around judgmental and critical people is not only exhausting, but also anxiety provoking. Sometimes it is hard to recognize an invalidator, because a truly good one can be very covert and underhanded. Sometimes they can trick you by giving you what I call a "slap-hug." This is when they give you a compliment and a criticism at the same time. Often it is masked by humor and if confronted they will say "Oh, I was just kidding!"

The way you know if you are being invalidated is by how you feel. Have you ever felt bad around someone without knowing why? Have you ever felt confused by something someone said to you? Have you ever felt like you were walking on eggshells around a particular person? This is probably because this person has been overtly or covertly judgmental of you.

You need to get away from judgmental people as much as possible. They will suppress you and cause you a great deal of anxiety. This anxiety will block your motivation. Not only that, but it if it goes too far, it will make you physically ill or cause you to get into accidents. Challenge the people in your life who are often critical. Ask them exactly what they mean. Usually there is an element of truth in criticism. Find the element of truth, agree to make necessary changes, then ask the person to let it go. Let people know that criticism is blocking your movement rather than furthering your action forward.

The people close to you are either bringing you up or bringing you down. You need to love yourself and value yourself enough that you will only allow positives into your life. We've all heard of "tough love" and how it relates to our relationships with people who are dragging us down. Yes, you need to get "tough love" with others on this issue. However, you also need to get use "tough love" with *yourself*, and follow these steps:

1. Determine who is bringing you up and who is bringing you down

2. Talk to those who often bring you down and ask for changes

3. If changes are not being made after several requests, detach from this person as much as possible

---

—No one can make you feel inferior without your permission.
                                                —Eleanor Roosevelt

Why Others Sabotage Us and How to Handle Them

Are you living the life YOU really want, or the life OTHERS want for you? This is a question you must ask yourself often. Your failure to handle this *one issue—sabotage by others*—can sabotage your entire achievement process!

Being too accommodating to others will impede your motivation. You give your power over to others when your effort toward your goals is contingent upon the participation and acceptance of other important people in your life. Moreover, it can be tempting to blame others for your own lack of movement, claiming that they will be jealous, angry, upset or overly needy if you succeed. It deprives you of your own power and autonomy. If it is others who are to blame for your failures, then these same others control your successes. This is giving away your power to others, and it is completely self-sabotaging.

One of the greatest needs of human beings is that of approval from others. Fear of disapproval is one of the greatest self-sabotages. When you are blocked because of fear of what others will think, focusing on the goal of "developing my true self" becomes a compelling replacement for the fear of "others' approval." According to Wayne Dyer, a truly self-actualized person is one who is not controlled by the opinions of others.

Dan Kennedy, a marketing and business consultant says, "Run, don't walk, I repeat RUN, DON'T WALK, from negative people!" But what if you *cannot* leave (or it is not in your overall best interest to leave) the people who are your greatest source of discouragement? James Prochaska (1995) discusses the idea of "enlisting" or "eliciting" helping relationships. He believes that helping relationships are of *primary value* to self changers. He says most people in your life do *want* to help you, but do *not know how* to help you! It is up to *you* to teach your family, friends, co-workers, roommates, etc. how they can be the most helpful. It is also helpful to find a good support person or support system aside from friends and family. Examples are personal coaches, counselors, support groups, sponsors, mentors, teachers, pastors, etc.

On the other hand, you may have "supporters" who exude tremendous pressure on you to achieve a particular goal, which may or may not be *your* goal. For example, the well-meaning mother who tells her daughter, "You know you really should go into interior design…you're very artistic…you have a gift…you shouldn't let it go to waste…" and so on. *Pressure creates resistance.* The more one is pressured to do something, the more difficult it seems to become. You need to set limits with people who pressure you, and again, teach them how to be supportive.

Now, here's one thing you can definitely count on. Once you've made the decision to go after your dreams, you WILL get RESISTANCE from certain people in your life! This is because seeing you go after your dreams (or making big changes) makes certain people feel uncomfortable. Why? One reason is because it reminds them that they have given up on their own dreams. They've joined the "I've given up on my dreams club," and they want you to be in their club. You've heard that old saying, "Misery loves company." They want to be where you are, and want you to be where they are. They are afraid of separation from you.

Another reason certain people are uncomfortable with you pursuing your goals is that they are afraid of what it might do to *you*. They are afraid it might change you. They are afraid you might fail. They are afraid you might succeed. Either way, some changes are going to happen, and it will have an effect on them. They do not want their "comfort zone" disturbed. This is the way they know you, and this is what is familiar, and this is what they want to continue to count on. Most people are afraid of change, which will be discussed at length in Chapter Thirteen: "I'm Afraid."

Having some empathy for others around us who will feel the effects of our changes is important. We need to enlist their support. We need to understand what they are feeling. We need to ask them what they are feeling. We need to ask for their support. It may just be the extra push that gets us through our difficult times and keeps us on our path to success.

—There is something about your success that even your best friend despises.

—Mark Twain

How to Handle Criticism Without Anguish

One thing is certain. *The more successful you get the more people are going to criticize you.* You need to be prepared for this criticism. Some criticism (constructive criticism) is good for us. It needs to be heeded for us to improve and grow. But what about criticism that is unwarranted? Some people just have a critical personality. It is important to be able to distinguish between warranted and unwarranted criticism. The best way to do this is to use evaluations and statistics.

Whenever I speak I always have at least one person give me critical comments on my evaluations. I honestly ask myself if this criticism was important, warranted, genuine, or worth listening to. If I'm not sure, I will ask a trusted colleague who knows my work and I know will be honest with me. I may ask several people their opinion so I can get an idea of what a "consensus" would think. Sometimes I learn something and make appropriate changes and am grateful someone took the risk to criticize me. Other times, I determine that this person may have been competitive, jealous, angry, in a bad mood, overly irritable, or simply coming from a different reality. Either way, I don't spend much time thinking about it. I get what I need to get, then move on.

I have learned that I cannot please all the people all the time. I can please most of the people most of the time. This is my goal. Not perfection—but simply to have a positive effect on as many people as I can. I used to be very sensitive to criticism. I have learned to deal with my sensitivity by what psychologists call "individuating." This is the realization that I am a separate person. I have independent thoughts, feelings, beliefs, opinions and ideas. Sometimes I have to detach, deflect, de-personalize, de-sensitize. While I realize that as human beings, we are all connected and have powerful effects on each other, I have learned that sometimes I just have to be *me*.

> —*How we spend our days is, of course, how we spend our lives.*
> —Annie Dillard

Choose Your People Well

The power of a support system cannot be emphasized enough. One only has to watch the "Academy Awards" and the celebrities who have climbed to the top of their profession (no easy feat!), and listen to their acceptance speeches. Rarely will they mention the difficulties, the processes, how they overcame their own sabotages and adversities—rather they spend their few moments thanking the people who supported them—and they all have them. Thanking people *in advance* for their support, validation and encouragement goes a long way in helping you achieve your goals.

When highly successful people are asked how they achieved their success they will almost always say something like, "I couldn't have done it without so-and-so." Do not underestimate the power of role models, coaches and mentors. This is why it is so important to choose your people well. The people in your life are either lifting you up or bringing you down. People can help make you or break you. You cannot afford the luxury of negative, counter, or limiting people around you. The people around you must support you, validate you and encourage you. I recently heard Angelina Jolie on a talk show say how important it is to her to have people in her life who "elevate" her. Find people with an attitude of "abundance" rather than an attitude of "deficit." More will be discussed on this topic in Chapter Sixteen: Social Aspects of Motivation.

—Do not allow anyone to cause you to lower your reach.
                                                        —Jeff Ribera

Exercise 12:1
Who Supports Me?

Your Personal Support Network

1. List the people that form the core of your social environment:

2. Next to each of their names, write how much time you generally spend with them per week, and then next to that, rate them on how much they support you and contribute to your well-being (rate them on a scale of 1–10, with 10 being the most supportive).

3. Sometimes, people give mixed messages. If this is the case with any of the people you listed above, write down how they do this.

4. Describe the ways in which your social network is lacking and then describe ways to improve it.

—We are each of us angels with only one wing, so we can only fly embracing each other.

—Luciano De Creshensa

Exercise 12:1
Promote Your Dream

On a separate piece of paper, write a promotional ad (or story) for the completion of one of your mission statements. List all of the benefits your idea has to offer, how the completion of this mission will help others, who it will help, why it will help better than any other mission. Lastly, ask for assistance, help, support for the achievement of your goals.

Share this promo with three people you trust. Write down their responses.

> —Keep your mind on the great and splendid thing you would like to do; and then, as the days go gliding by, you will find yourself unconsciously seizing the opportunities that are required for the fulfillment of your desire...Picture in your mind the able, earnest, useful person you desire to be, and the thought that you hold is hourly transforming you into that particular individual you so admire.
>
> —Elbert Hubbard

Chapter Thirteen:
Self-Sabotage #7: "I'm Afraid"

Fear—The Biggest Obstacle

Fear. It is by far the number one saboteur of success. Most people fear the unknown. They fear change. They fear failure, success, disapproval, criticism, pain and struggle. Fear keeps people persisting in unhappy and dysfunctional situations, because they know that changing the situation will lead to the unknown, which may be even more painful than what they are currently experiencing. Your fears may be rational or irrational. They need to be examined in the context of reality to determine how great the risk really is. You need to determine whether the changes you are considering are likely to increase your likelihood of a more satisfying, happier life.

Most fears that inhibit motivation stem from low self-esteem. In this regard, the fear of failure and the fear of success are integrally connected. Atkinson's *Michigan Studies of Fear and Failure* states that the tendency to avoid failure seems to dampen the effort to perform well. Consequently, fearing failure is counter-productive, since it essentially furthers the likelihood of failure. For some, the fear of failure is so great that it seems safer not to attempt anything at all. Often such people have experienced a failure that felt devastating and that they haven't worked through. Attempting something new is thus viewed as taking the risk of repeating such a crushing disappointment.

—We should not let our fears hold us back from pursuing our hopes.
—John F. Kennedy

The One Change You Need to Make in Your Head

There are ways of mentally restructuring your thoughts to put fears into a new perspective. Try substituting the phrase "learning experience" for "failure." For example, instead of saying, "I failed to win the tennis match," try, "I learned that when playing this opponent, I should hit the ball to her backhand more often." This will give you a new goal for the next time you play, rather than making you anxious and fearful of defeat before you even begin the match.

Another rephrasing technique is to look at "failure" as a particular *event* in which you did not achieve your desired outcome. Often, the danger of believing in failure is that people tend to generalize: "I failed, therefore I'm a failure." If you put the failure into perspective as a single event, rather than a life sentence, you will not sabotage your future attempts to reach the goal. Likewise, the purpose of using the phrase "learning experience" is to realize that what seems like a failure is not an end to everything, but part of a larger *growth process*. This concept can be similarly applied to success, since ideally successes are not ending points but milestones en route to other successes. In a competitive society we can be brainwashed into thinking that everything is either a win or a loss. Right vs. wrong. One up vs. one down. Good vs. bad. We need to refrain from this type of good-bad "splitting" and transfer to more positive thoughts.

—The master key to riches, is thought by thought, replace old negative thoughts with new positive thoughts.

—Napoleon Hill

Rational or Irrational?

Fear is with us for a reason. It protects us from danger. However, many times our fears are overly intense and not based in reality. If you want to deal with an irrational fear, you may want to do research on the goals at which you fear you will fail. Through research, you can to some extent, determine the likelihood of success and assess whether your fears are founded. For instance, if you are afraid of applying to a particular graduate school, you can look at statistics on what percentage of applicants are accepted into the program, what percentage of those accepted complete the program, and what percentage of those that complete the program successfully find jobs.

Another way to assess your likelihood of success or failure is to ask ten people who know you well what they think of your ability to achieve a particular goal. If all or most of them say they think it is an unrealistic goal, this should tell you something. On the other hand, if all or most of them feel strongly that you could achieve this goal, it is likely they are correct. Having supportive, caring, familiar people help us to analyze our risk is a more objective method than determining our risk all by ourselves.

Like the fear of failure, the fear of criticism and the fear of change lead to inaction, since that is the safer route. Fear of success occurs when a person has such self-doubt that success brings with it overwhelming anxiety—a sense that the success is not deserved, that it cannot last, and that disaster is imminent. Often in such cases, people will purposefully destroy the success so as to end the anxiety that accompanies it. This is about the feeling that *known* failure is better than the prolonged *anticipation* of failure. We know too well the scenario of those who rose to the top so rapidly, and so unprepared, that they self-medicated their anxiety with drugs and/or alcohol (often to their own demise).

The fears of failure and success are blocks that, with patience and time, can be confronted and overcome. Once success has been proven with respect to small, simple tasks, the individual's confidence increases and the fear of failure diminishes because success has been proven. Take for example the reclusive, awkwardly shy teenage boy who gets his first job and suddenly begins to express himself more freely. The act of undertaking the pursuit of a goal can in itself build self-esteem, whether or not the goal itself is eventually achieved. You may be pleasantly surprised to see that as you become increasingly confident about your abilities, you become ready to take on larger challenges.

Psychological studies have shown that people may regret actions more than inactions at first, but over a longer period of time they come to regret inactions more than actions. One study found that when elderly people were asked about their greatest lifetime regrets, 63 percent of the regrets were about inaction. Just knowing this statistic can help you overcome fears and doubts about your own action and feel more ready to take risks and pursue your goals.

—At this point in my life I'm very self-assured about what I want and where I'm going. I have this quote in my diary that I stick to: 'I do not intend to tiptoe through life only to arrive safely at death.'
—Christina Aguilera

10 Tips for Handling Worry and Anxiety

Worry is a self-defeating behavior. It will take years off your life, will wreak havoc with your emotional health, and won't solve your problems. In fact, it interferes with your ability to make good decisions. Change the word *WORRIER* to *WARRIOR*. Change the words "I'm a worrier" to "I'm a warrior!" Change the thought "I worry too much" to "I used to worry; now I give it over to my higher power." Change the thought "I'm so worried that…" to "It's so unlikely to happen, and I have no control over it anyway, that I'm choosing to let it go."

Awfulizing and catastrophizing are the supreme self sabotages. The great French philosopher Montaigne once wrote, "My life has been full of terrible misfortunes, most of which never happened." Anxiety distorts normal worries and magnifies them. Anxiety can be a terrible curse or an enormous blessing. It can propel us into action or it can paralyze us from movement. It can save our lives or it can cause our demise. So, assess your anxiety level and use the following techniques to reduce your anxiety.

The following are 10 tips for handling anxiety:

1. Keep a journal. Each day, before going to sleep, write down 5 to 10 things for which you are grateful for that day.
2. Practice random anonymous acts of kindness.
3. Face your fears—they are not as terrible as you imagine.
4. Recognize how the anxiety keeps you immobilized.
5. Acknowledge your amazing potential and strive to maximize it every day.
6. Intend on being peaceful, relaxed and calm.
7. Ask yourself "what's the worst that can happen?" Then ask "what are the chances of that happening?" If the chances are minimal, "fagetabottit!"
8. Recite the serenity prayer.
9. Let go and let God.
10. Breathe.

—A ship in a safe harbor is safe, but that is not what a ship is built for.
—William Shedd

Exercise 13:1
What Has Stopped Me in the Past?

Self-sabotage and Fear

Sometimes we suffer from anxiety and sabotage your efforts at success because of hidden beliefs and fears that we did not even know we had. Self pressure and perfectionism are common blockers of motivation and change.

Complete the following sentences as a way of exploring these hidden thoughts and fears:

I <u>have to</u> be perfect at _____ .
I <u>need</u> to please_____ .
I <u>should</u> be able to do more_____ .
I've <u>got</u> to prove that_____ .
I <u>ought</u> to finish_____ .
I <u>must</u> take care of_____ .
I <u>should</u> be happy because_____ .

   Now, consider the underlined words in each previous sentence. These hidden feelings cause guilt and anxiety. In the following sentences, the underlined words have been replaced with positive feelings not associated with guilt, pressure or a sense of duty. See how your answers differ in this exercise:

I <u>want to</u> be good at _____ .
I <u>want</u> to please_____ .
I <u>would like to</u> be able to do more_____ .
I <u>want to</u> show that_____ .
I <u>would like</u> to finish_____ .
I <u>hope to</u> take care of_____ .
I <u>aspire</u> to be happy because_____ .

—Courage is not the absence of fear, rather the mastery of fear.
                                                    —Dan Rather

Exercise 13:2
Disputing Irrational Beliefs

Write down an irrational belief that you hold, such as "I must be absolutely sure before I make a decision":

Can you think of any support for this idea?

What evidence is there to support the falseness of this idea?

What is the worst thing that could happen if you hold on to this idea?

What positive things could happen if you gave up this idea?

What are some alternative thoughts that might allow you to try more things and feel better about yourself?

—When you say you fear death, you're really saying that you fear you haven't lived your true life. What is your true life? That which makes you happy.

—David Viscott

Part III:

STICKING WITH IT

Chapter Fourteen:
Enduring the Struggle

Setbacks and Adversity

As you have seen, the most important aspects of progress are positive thoughts, social support, and enduring the struggle. This chapter is about how to endure the struggle. They say, "When the going gets tough, the tough get going." But how do you develop that toughness to keep going? Sometimes you need to move even when you don't feel motivated at all. How do you keep moving when you don't feel like it at all?

First, you realize that there *will* be adversity along the way. There will be setbacks, obstacles, challenges, delays. You already predicted it, you expected it, and when it comes it is no surprise to you. Prepare for setbacks and problems. Put a plan in place ahead of time so you will know how to deal with them. Do not become discouraged when you encounter them along the way. Remember times when you achieved success in the past after enduring hardships. Remind yourself how you were able to overcome obstacles and endure frustration in the past. These memories will serve to be very powerful motivators in getting through the low and slow times.

One of the ways I deal with setbacks, obstacles and problems (I call them "glitches" now) is by staying ahead of my game most of the time. I try to stay ahead of schedule, even if just a little. For example, if I want to get 1, 2, and 3 done by Friday, I go ahead and get 4 done by Friday as well. Now I'm ahead of schedule. Psychologically, this helps to ease my anxiety or anticipation of "problems." It's like having money in a savings account for the unexpected or emergency situation. In the same way, you can put time into your savings account by working ahead on your goals. If a "problem" arises, you know you can handle a delay. If you get sick or just don't feel like doing anything for a while, you will not veer off schedule too far.

—*When you face the sun, the shadows always fall behind you.*
                                                    —Helen Keller

Accepting the Unexpected

Life is about change. It is constantly changing. One day we think we have a handle on life, and the next day the handle breaks. Just when we think we've made ends meet, they move the ends. Often, change fires itself at us point blank. It doesn't wait until we are ready. Therefore, the ability to remain flexible and to moderate and/or modify our goals is a trait worth adopting.

If you have a spiritual belief that the Universe is working for your highest good, it will be much easier to accept things that do not go your way. We've all experienced times when we went through a very painful experience and thought our world was falling apart. Then after time had passed we discovered that experience was a Godsend. When someone or something "throws a wrench" in my plans, I try to realize that this may just be a blessing in disguise. This may just be "the best, worst thing" that ever happened to me. I often quote the popular phrase, "Every cloud has a silver lining."

Enduring the struggle requires altering our usual routines and ways of thinking. It often involves change on our parts. It involves a change in our thoughts, our words, our attitudes, our actions, and even our personality. It involves the ability to adapt, modify, and be flexible. It involves a tremendous amount of patience.

The more advantages one has in these areas, the easier it will be for change to occur. Each individual possesses personal traits that will enable him/her to develop motivation and more importantly, to remain motivated, especially in the face of adversity. However, fewer advantages should not be used as an excuse NOT to change. Although you may feel, for instance, that you can't change the fact that you were brought up poor without the advantages that others have, you do have control over your attitude and your perceptions of how much you will allow your past to influence your future. In this case, you might want to study examples of people who overcame meager beginnings and went on to be very successful.

—Life is a grindstone, and whether it grinds you down or polishes you up is for you and you alone to decide.

—Cavett Robert

The Real Reason People Procrastinate and How to Overcome It

You may be like most people and struggle from time to time with procrastination. You may wonder why you or others procrastinate. Procrastination comes in many forms, such as not making decisions, being late to events, not showing up, putting things off till the last minute, not completing projects, not putting things away, not cleaning up after oneself, etc. It is caused by many different things, such as laziness, selfishness, stubbornness, passive resistance, rebellion, fear, perfectionism, etc.

Surprisingly, research shows the number one cause of procrastination is the *need to be perfect*. Perfectionists suffer tremendous psychological and emotional pain. They are constantly "in a bind." They are damned if they do, damned if they don't. They can't decide and act because there is no perfect decision. There are just different choices with different possible outcomes. Perfectionists tend to see the worst thing that could happen in any choice, therefore resisting action based on such horrible possible outcomes. They can't see any good way to go, so they do nothing.

What procrastinators don't realize is that NOT making a decision IS making a decision! They are making an unconscious choice to do nothing. They may give lots of excuses, justifications, and rationalizations for their lack of movement, but the reality is, it was their choice. Being around a procrastinator is just as frustrating (if not more so) as being a procrastinator.

If perfectionism is the cause of the person's procrastination, this can be handled by asking the person what is their greatest fear or worst case scenario. Then, using REBT (Rational Emotive Behavior Therapy) principles, ask them what the possibility is of that worst thing happening. Reduce their anxiety by talking about their worst fear, and the reality of it's slim chance of happening, and the reality of it not being so bad if it did happen, thereby de-sensitizing them to it. Then ask them what the possibility is of the best thing happening, and have them describe that. Ask them to take a risk and make a decision.

If the procrastination is caused by laziness, resistance, or some other such reason, simply remind the person of the payoff for doing what they don't really want to do. We all have things to do every day that we don't particularly like doing. I often don't feel like getting up when my alarm goes off in the morning. I often don't feel like taking a shower and getting dressed, driving to work, doing certain tasks, household chores, etc. Yet I do them because of the positive result I receive for doing them. Sometimes just pointing out the consequences for procrastination vs. getting it done now can give them the extra push.

Setting firm limits and boundaries, such as stating "I need this finished by 2PM today" can also be helpful. When verbal limits do not work, putting our limits in writing can add the necessary push. If the person still does not respond, you will need to determine what you will do, such as, "If you are not ready by 6:00 I will go without you."

A great way to overcome procrastination is to make whatever it is that needs to be done YOUR CHOICE. Make it your choice to do it. Rather than resenting that you must do it, or feeling guilty about the fact that you should do it, simply choose to do it. From all the available possibilities, choose what you know is right. Knowing you are doing the RIGHT thing will often overcome all obstacles. Choose, and then put the power and commitment of your intention behind your actions. When you choose to do it, you put yourself in positive control of your own destiny. You make yourself vastly more effective.

I used to be terrified of roller coasters and other amusement park rides. I would get nauseous and sick on these rides. I really wanted to get over my fear because my young daughter loved nothing more than these rides and I wanted to be able to go on them with her. Someone told me that the way to get over my fear was to imagine I was in control of the ride—that I was actually the driving force, making the ride go up and down and sideways and upside down. I tried this, and to my amazement it worked!

When you feel that you are forced or obligated to do something, it makes you feel like you have no choice and you will naturally resist it. So choose to do it and free yourself from these useless burdens. Choose to do it not because you must, not because you should, but because you know it is right and best for YOU. Every moment is a choice. In every moment, in every situation, make it your choice to do what is best. Make it YOUR choice and you'll make it great!

—Hard work pays off later, laziness pays off now.

—Unknown

Others who Overcame Adversity

As outlined previously, having role models of people who have overcome adversity will greatly assist you in enduring your own struggle. Recalling these stories is an excellent way to work through blocks in your progress. It is helpful to have a model of a person (or several people) with whom you can identify: someone who has had similar struggles and has overcome them. It makes us think, if so-and-so could do it, why can't I? The stories have the effect of making you identify with a community of survivors, of confident people who believed in themselves and achieved success because of their determination. Following are some sample stories:

   * Thomas Muster, an Austrian professional tennis player, was ranked sixth in the world. He had just won the semi-finals of the Lipton International Tennis Tournament and was scheduled to play in the men's finals the next day. That night, while putting his tennis bag in the trunk of his car, a drunk driver hit him and shattered his knee so badly that after his surgery, the doctors told him he might never walk again. He did come back, however, and was able to rise back up to his sixth place ranking in the world. Muster's story demonstrates the importance of being adaptive as well as determined. Muster's life was clearly changed by his accident, but rather than succumbing to this setback, he adapted to the new circumstances with even greater determination.

   *Lance Armstrong was ranked the #1 cyclist in the world in 1995. He was on his way to reaching his goal of winning the Tour de France bicycling race when, in 1996 at the age of 25, he was diagnosed with advanced testicular cancer that had spread to his lungs and brain. Undergoing major surgery and heavy chemotherapy treatments, he beat the odds and survived. By 1999 he was ready to race again. The sponsors of his old racing team had given up on him, but he never gave up on himself. He convinced another sponsor, the United States Postal Service, to back him and went on to win the Tour de France a record breaking seven consecutive times. He also started the *Lance Armstrong Foundation* which, through its sale of yellow "Livestrong" rubber bracelets and other donations, has made tens of millions of dollars for cancer research.

   *Ronan Tynan, was born with focamelia, a congenital deformity, yet he trained as a competitive horseback rider and jumper as a boy. At the age of 20 he had both of his legs amputated below the knee and went on to win 19 gold medals and set 14 world records in the Paralympic Games. He obtained several educational degrees, became a medical doctor as well as a world famous singer and member of The Irish Tenors.

—Endurance is one of the most difficult disciplines, but it is to the one who endures that the final victory comes.

—Buddha

Using Life Traumas or Difficulties as Motivators

As the anecdotes about Muster and Armstrong exemplify, life traumas have the potential to work as motivators rather than inhibitors. One almost always encounters obstacles in the pursuit of one's goals. Overcoming obstacles—particularly large ones—proves one's determination and makes one's attainment of the final goal that much more meaningful. In *Imperfect Control* (1998), Judith Viorst writes,

> *Studies of victimization have found that most of us, until we have been victimized, share three basic, often unconscious, assumptions:*
>> *We assume that we are personally invulnerable.*
>> *We assume that the world we live in is comprehensible.*
>> *We assume that we are essentially worthwhile.*
> *Victimization deprives us of this sense of certainty.*

As the title of Viorst's book suggests, no one is always in control of life. The assumptions that Viorst lists as characterizing people who have never been victimized suggest an attitude of taking life for granted. Although it is certainly not to be wished for, the experience of trauma can thus lead to increased motivation, because it robs one of these assumptions, forcing one to reevaluate what in life is important and what is worth pursuing. Lance Armstrong demonstrates this by saying that having cancer was an unexpected gift—"the best thing that ever happened to me," because it caused him to rethink his priorities. He never lost sight of his goal to win the Tour de France, but he also began to see good health, something he had always taken for granted—and a loving family and good friends—as blessings.

The notion of hardship, as leading to increased motivation, is affirmed in Gail Sheehy's *Pathfinders*. She writes,

> *Repeated to a striking degree in the histories of the most satisfied adults was a history of a troubled period during late childhood or adolescence, when many rated themselves as very unhappy...Anyone who overcomes a difficult childhood is likely to acquire that key characteristic—a concentration of optimism—and quite possibly an orientation toward the present and future rather than an emphasis on the past.*

It is not what happens to us that influences our motivation so much as our *perceptions* of what happens and the manner in which we choose to act in response. In terms of thought transformation, perpetual victims see life in terms of "Why me?" and "I can't, because..." whereas recovering victims see life in terms of "What can I do with this?" Unhappiness and discomfort can be calls to action.

Furthermore, significant emotional events often are able to change our behavior (or motivate us to act) more than insight or any other thought. For example, a man has known for a long time that he should write a living will. Yet he puts it off until he is almost killed in a car accident.

Life is like driving down a long, winding road. You never know what the next curve will bring—a beautiful view or a dangerous pothole. One thing is certain though. As long as you're alive, you're still moving forward and eventually you'll leave the obstacles behind. Unwelcome detours finally do end, and easier stretches lie ahead. You eventually do get to your destination. And you will have learned more from your journeys than from lying around safely at home.

—In the middle of difficulty lies opportunity.
—Albert Einstein

Exercise 14:1
"What Am I Willing To Do To Get It?"

Write down a particular goal:

Now, assess the **obstacles** you may encounter while pursuing this goal:

Fears   Ways to Overcome Fears

Resources Commonly Felt Lacking   Ways to Overcome Each Impediment

Time

Money

Skill/Talent

Other Obstacles   Ways to Overcome

Worst Case Scenario   Best Case Scenario

—...*to be measured not so much by the position that one has reached in life as by the obstacles which he has overcome while trying to succeed.*

—Booker T. Washington

Exercise 14:2
How Am I Doing?
Assessing Progress

Draw a picture—for example, a mountain, a set of stairs, or a thermometer—that will enable you to measure your progress. Write out your goal and the steps involved in reaching it along the side of the picture. You can refer back to this picture each week and mark off your progress. As the picture is gradually filled in, you will feel a building sense of accomplishment.

Example:

GOAL:

Steps:
_____
_____
_____

GOAL:

Steps:
_____
_____
_____

GOAL:

Steps:
_____
_____
_____

GOAL:

Steps:
_____
_____
_____

—In order to succeed, you must know what you are doing, like what you are doing, and believe in what you are doing.
—Will Rogers

Chapter Fifteen:
Thought and Attitude Transformation

How to Develop Ambition

Ambition is a critical component of achievement. In order to pursue one's life goals, one must first become ambitious. This means breaking out of the comfortable familiarity of routine which is called the "comfort zone." But how does one get ambition?

Steven Scott describes the process of developing ambition in terms of an "awakening": realizing that we have been "programmed for mediocrity" and then realizing that this prior programming does not doom us to continuing to abide by this mediocrity. As Sarah Breathnach argues in her book *Simple Abundance* (1995), perhaps ambition is already within us:

> *Ambition is achievement's soul mate. Action is the matchmaker that brings these affinities together so that sparks can begin to fly and we can set the world on fire…Just as electricity can be life enhancing or destructive, so can ambition. What ambition really needs is a new press agent. The only time we ever hear about her is when she's blamed for somebody's downfall…But what if we are supposed to be ambitious? What if our refusal to channel our ambitions for our highest good, the highest good of those we love and the rest of the world, is the real corruption of Power? Think of all that could be accomplished if women cherished their ambitions and brought them into the Light where they belong. Think of how our lives could be transformed if we respected ambition and gave grateful thanks for being entrusted with such a miraculous gift.*

According to Breathnach's theory, we can assume that if we are lacking ambition, then it has been suppressed. The challenge then, is to bring to light the ambition that is within us. This ambition may be difficult to find, as it may have been squelched for many years. Often, however, all it takes is for you to give yourself *permission* to bring it up. In order to counter the common tendency to think of ambition, or drive, as a negative characteristic, you should consider ambition as a positive attribute—a gift—when used for good, in the pursuit of your goals. Once your ideas about ambition have been transformed into a positive framework, you may find you encounter a motivational breakthrough.

Developing healthy ambition is often about finding a balance. Optimistic thinking has proven to be a major factor in self-motivation. Nonetheless, most of us know people who are over-optimistic and over-ambitious. These people are often called "dreamers" or "serial enthusiasts." They move from place to place, job to job, relationship to relationship, hobby to hobby, each time announcing that "THIS IS THE ONE!"

People who are too ambitious often have over-ambitious goals as well as over-ambitious time lines. They only feel good if they achieve large goals, so they lose sight of the smaller goals. They are too impatient to work on the smaller sub-goals and the often, tedious steps involved in getting to the larger goals. This is why they are constantly changing directions. As soon as the process begins to get difficult, or frustrating, or seems to take too long or is too much work, they move on to the next "great idea." Do you often find yourself stopping progress on a certain goal because "I've changed my mind?" If that seems to happen repeatedly each time you are striving to reach a particular goal, you need to assess if what you are really saying is, "It got too hard," or "It's taking too long."

—Real courage is when you know you're licked before you begin, but you begin anyway and see it through no matter what.

—Harper Lee

Optimism vs. Pessimism— Why the Big Deal?

On the other hand, pessimists worry about doing things perfectly and never seem able to make a move. They continually use their imagination to visualize worst case scenarios, and then conclude that those scenarios are so probable, and the effects are so hopeless that there is no cause for action.

On a continuum between overly optimistic and overly pessimistic, there is a healthy medium. Healthy people who find themselves thinking too optimistically or pessimistically will challenge their own thoughts. They will look at both sides of the coin and debate them until they feel they have a realistic idea of how to proceed. If this course of action does not achieve the desired results, they will alter or modify it until it does. It is important to become a realist, to get to a point between over-optimism and pessimism where you can debate the pros and cons of various actions and assess likely outcomes.

Ambition usually does not spring up automatically. Often, you must use self discipline rather than depend on intrinsic (internal) motivation in order to begin a task. But, if you can develop the discipline to begin, motivation will often follow. External (extrinsic) motivation can be internalized, and with the passage of time, as you adjust to new tasks and become pleased with the results of new successes, intrinsic motivation will develop.

One way to develop ambition and motivation is to first act "as if." When you start acting and behaving like the successful person you want to become, the feelings tend to follow. Acting "as if" causes you to create new habits, and soon you will find that they are natural to you. You may soon find other people commenting on your new habit, such as "how patient you are." You know that it took years of practice, of acting "as if" for you to develop that trait, so you may respond, "I haven't always been this way—it took a lot of hard work."

—Acting as if you were already what you want to become and knowing that you can become it is the way to remove self-doubt and enter your real-magic kingdom.

—Wayne Dyer

Controlled Focus is Your Laser Beam to Success

Tony Robbins, one of the greatest contributors to motivational thought transformation in the self-help movement, writes, "In order to succeed, you must have a long term focus." He believes that in order to gain any valuable, long term pleasure, one must break through some short-term pain. This begins with the *decision* to overcome the discomfort of short-term pain. Robbins speaks of the principle of "concentration of power" or "controlled focus." He believes that people can achieve more than they realize when they focus their intentions on their goals. His delineation of the thought transformation process involves three steps:

1) Raise Your Standards: Decide what you will accept and what you will not accept for your life.

2) Change Your Limiting Beliefs: Develop a sense of confidence that you can, and will, meet your new standards.

3) Change Your Strategy: The best strategy is to find a role model, someone who is already getting the results you want, and tap into their knowledge.

"Your life changes," says Robbins, "the moment you make a *new, congruent, and committed* decision." Brian Tracy reiterates Robbins' point about long term focus in *Secrets of Success* (1997) and goes on to emphasize the feelings of confidence, mastery, and self-esteem that ensue when one achieves sustained concentration.

The famous entrepreneur and philanthropist, Andrew Carnegie believed strongly in "controlled focus", although the term was not coined until long after his death. After his family moved from Scotland to the United States, he went to work as a bobbin boy in a cotton mill at the age of thirteen. He later established his own business enterprises, eventually organizing the Carnegie Steel Company. At the age of 65, he sold the company for $480 million. His thoughts on "focus" can be seen in his quote on ultimate success, *"Here is the prime condition of success, the great secret—concentrate your energy, thought and capital exclusively upon the business in which you are engaged. Having begun on one line, resolve to fight it out on that line, to lead in it, adopt every improvement, have the best machinery and know the most about it. Finally, do not be impatient, for as Emerson says, 'No one can cheat you out of ultimate success but yourself'."*

Another way to stick with your dreams is to saturate yourself with information about your dreams. For example, if you desire to become a famous actress, read everything you can about acting. Get every book and subscribe to every magazine you can find on the subject. Watch every television program on how famous actors got where they are. Read every biography you can find on famous actors. Go see as many actors in person as you can. Go to their websites and study them. Attend their "chat sessions" online. Take as many acting classes as you can. The more you know about your goal the more it will feel like a part of you. The more it feels like a part of you, the more confidence you will have that you can do it.

Along this line, it is important to mention *practice*. A famous athlete once said, "Those who love their craft, love the practice." If you don't love practicing, you will probably never be that good at it. So practice, practice, practice!

—When you get into a tight place and everything goes against you, till it seems you could not hold on a minute longer, never give up then, for that is just the place and time that the tide will turn.
—Harriet Beecher Stowe

Your Words are Your Power

Your word is the power you have to create. Your word is the power you have to motivate yourself. Words can literally change our beings and our actions. In her book, *The Right Words at the Right Time*, Marlo Thomas provides a wonderful expose of the words that motivated a variety of people who have achieved great things. She discusses how words have a tremendous impact on us. They can either serve to move us to action or to keep us down. For example, she quotes:

> *"Muhammad Ali responded to a teacher's assertion that he 'ain't never gonna be nuthin'. Billy Crystal, Walter Cronkite, Katie Couric and Kenneth Cole also received words of discouragement that goaded them on to achievement. The right words moved Al Pacino to pull out of a downward spiral. Paul McCartney's words came in a dream; Steven Spielberg's came from Davey Crockett. Chris Rock's words, like mine, came from his father; Supreme Court Justice Ruth Bader Ginsburg's from her mother-in-law on the eve of her wedding. Rudolph Giuliani, Cindy Crawford and Gwyneth Paltrow heard the words that changed their lives during a moment of crisis."*

Some positive self statements come to us naturally, and some are much more difficult to fuse into our being. One of the words I often use is "intention." Intention is what we want to have happen—our primary objective—our true aim. When I wake up in the morning I think about how I want my day to go. I say "My intention today is to be safe, happy and healthy, and to complete one chapter in my book." My day usually goes according to my intention. However, sometimes it seems the whole world is conspiring against my intention. Lots of distractions come up, people don't do what they are supposed to do, things are delayed for reasons beyond my control, things break down and I have to stop and fix them, etc. I have to be flexible and patient during these times.

Usually however, what stops my intention is my own refusal to set limits with others. People distract me and get me off my course by either asking for my help, or attempting to engage me in THEIR problems/crises/dramas. This is where I am weakest, as I am by nature a people-helper. So what I have learned to do (when possible) is to tell (not ask) others what my intentions are, and that after my intentions have been met, I will be available to them. By the time I'm ready for them, they have usually solved their own problem!

Sometimes, with certain people, I have to change the word "intend" to "insist." Sometimes it's okay to insist that things go your way. As long as you are not stepping on anyone else's toes, or harming anyone else, or neglecting to care for those who really need you, you have the right to insist on doing your own thing, i.e. getting to your appointment on time or completing your goal on time.

You can use the list of words in Exercise 15:1 as "reward words" to yourself. For example, if you have just accomplished something that was a challenge for you, pat yourself on the back and say "Wow, that really took perseverance, but I did it." It is very important to remind yourself often of how far you've come in your journey.

—Life is a rush into the unknown. You can duck down and hope nothing hits you, or stand up tall as you can, show it your teeth and say "Bring it on, Baby, and don't be stingy with the jalapenos!"

—Anonymous

Exercise 15:1
Words as Motivational Tools

The following are useful words to incorporate in thought transformation with examples of how to use them. After each example, write your own positive affirmation related to each word. Then think of more words you can use to describe yourself on your journey of goal achievement.

Focus: I am focused on my driving so I will not be distracted.

_____
_____
_____

Concentration: I have excellent concentration for 90 minutes at a time.

_____
_____
_____

Intention: My intention is to lose 6 pounds within three months.

_____
_____
_____

Willpower: I use my willpower to exercise daily even when I don't feel like it.

_____
_____
_____

Dedication: I am dedicated to completing this job and I will not give up on it.

_____
_____
_____

Persistence: My persistence in getting a promotion will eventually pay off.

_____
_____
_____

Perseverance: I can persevere through setbacks and challenging times.

_____
_____
_____

Commitment: I am committed to making this happen and getting others to support me.

_____

_____

Determination: I am determined to get my degree, no matter how long it takes.

_____

_____

Courage: I have courage to continue, even when it seems hopeless.

_____

_____

_____

Other words:

_____

_____

_____

_____

_____

_____

_____

_____

_____

_____

—*When you change the way you look at something, that something will change the way it looks.*

—Wayne Dyer

Exercise 15:2
Replacing Negative Self-Statements

Think about the self-deprecating, counter-productive statements that you tend to say to yourself, such as "I'm bored," "This is too hard," or "This will never work." If you can consciously shift your thought to more positive ones, you are more likely to stick with projects and feel good about your involvement in them. Research has shown that people who think more positively tend to accomplish more goals and stay healthier. So, when you catch yourself thinking negative statements, stop the thought and immediately replace it with a positive one, such as "I've already made progress, and if I stick with it, I know I can succeed."

Negative Statement: Positive Statement:
Ex: "I can't take karate because I'm   "I can choose to take karate. I can get
out of shape and it's too hard to get to   in shape as I go. I can schedule time to
the studio 3 X a week."   go."

_____   _____
_____   _____
_____   _____
_____   _____
_____   _____
_____   _____
_____   _____

—Turn your "test" into a "testimony" and turn your "mess" into a "message."
                                                              —Unknown

Chapter Sixteen:
Social Aspects of Motivation

Fly in "V" Formation

Research shows that we are shaped largely by our interactions with others. Whether we have a long conversation with a friend or simply place an order at a restaurant, every interaction makes a difference. The results of our encounters are rarely neutral; they are almost always positive or negative. Remember, motivation is based mostly on "VEE"—*Values, Enjoyment and Empowerment.* When I think of "VEE" I think of a flock of geese flying in their traditional "V" formation. Engineers have learned that each bird, by flapping its wings, creates an uplift for the bird that follows. Together the whole flock gains about 70 percent greater flying range than if they were journeying alone.

In pursuing your goals, especially difficult ones, you cannot afford the luxury of a negative thought! You must devote a huge amount of your energy to motivating yourself and pursuing your goal. You don't have enough energy to ward off negative energy and still pursue your goal with fervor.

If you feel someone is not giving you the support you would like in pursuit of your new goals, you should first assess whether their doubts are valid. Is it possible that these doubts are legitimate and that your goals are either too rushed, problematic or unrealistic? If this is not the case, and you feel that they are not being supportive due to other reasons, you should discuss this with them, but you should not allow their discomfort to stand in the way of you achieving your goals.

This being said, you need to know that the people who are close to you usually do want to support you but don't know how. You need to teach them how. You may need to give them the exact step-by-step process to use. Above all, I ask the people closest to me to be supportive, validating and encouraging. If they slip into negativity, I simply imagine I have a mirror in front of me and their words bounce off me and reflect back onto them. I state, "I only hear positives."

It is imperative for your success that you surround yourself with positive thinkers. It is difficult enough to be a positive thinker, so without encouragement and validation from others your progress will be impeded. Ask others in your life to "catch" you when you slip into negative thinking and self-doubt. Ask them to force you to restate your words into a more positive statement. Ask them to remind you of how far you've come and how much you have already accomplished.

—*Once you've done the mental work, there comes a point you have to throw yourself into the action and put your heart on the line. That means not only being brave, but being passionate towards yourself, your teammates and your opponents.*

—Phil Jackson

Partners and Teams

Partnering and teamwork can also lead to greater motivation if you *truly* feel committed to the other team members. Even for someone with a low sense of self-esteem, she/he can go beyond these self-doubts because of her/his desire to succeed not only for her/himself but for the other members of the team. Having a partner can increase the motivation of both people, because they can profit from each other's energy and motivation. The partnership that is formed is a larger unit than the self. Each partner then becomes committed to, and will feel responsible for, this larger unit. The only caveat is that each of the partners should maintain a level of independence. Without this level of independence, a dysfunctional relationship will most likely arise.

Unlike mentoring or coaching, partnering should be a balanced relationship. In the corporate setting, more emphasis is now being placed on "teamwork" and creation of "working teams." This concept has been shown to be much more productive than when workers previously worked in isolation in their cubicles. Team members can provide additional motivation and support; however, they can also impede progress if they have a negative attitude. Team members can become more united and less irritated with each other if they keep their focus on their shared goals.

It is important to point out that people are very different in regard to their need for social support. Some people need much more social support than others do: some individuals work better alone, others work better as part of a team. It is vital when partnering that you determine what your needs are in the area of social support, and whether or not those needs can be met.

The movie "Alive" is based on the amazing, true story of a South American rugby team whose plane crashed in the Andes en route to a tournament in Santiago. Those few who survived said their courage came not only from their fear of death but also their will to see their families again. Emphasizing the social component of motivation, they all stated that it was the constant encouragement of their teammates that forced them to stay alive.

—Strange is our situation here on earth—we are here for a short visit—why? I don't know. I sense a divine calling that I am here for the sake of other humans and unknown soldiers whose fate is connected by a bond of sympathy.

—Albert Einstein

Role Models

As we discussed previously, role models can be an integral part of developing confidence with respect to new goals. For instance, a Latina student who will be the first person in her family to go to college will have a greater sense of confidence about her ability to succeed if she is introduced to a supportive Latina who comes from a similar background, has successfully completed college, and has embarked on a rewarding career based on her academic success in college.

Doing research for role models can help with your motivation. If you know of someone personally who you admire and who has achieved something similar to what you are striving for, ask them how they did it. What techniques did they employ? What were their challenges along the way? How did they overcome obstacles or fears? You'll be surprised at how receptive most people are to discussing their success with you.

Role models are extremely powerful motivators. They are worth their weight in gold. However, as with all human beings, they are imperfect. They are fallible, and may mess up their lives at times. Many professional athletes have let down their young idols by getting involved in drugs, adultery, and other criminal or unethical behaviors. If your role models let you down in some way, learn from their mistakes and move on. Find role models who have learned from their own past mistakes as well as the past mistakes of their own peers and role models.

> —*If I can do it, so can you. When I speak I don't want people to leave saying, "She's great." I want them to leave saying "If she can do it, so can I!"*
> —Lyn Kelley

Mentors, Sponsors and Teachers

Mentors, sponsors and teachers are more pots of gold for you. They play a critical role in helping people overcome hardship and adversity. Alcoholics Anonymous uses a sponsor system in which new members are matched with sponsors who have had similar experiences and who have overcome similar problems. In *Pathfinders* (1981), her detailed study of people who succeed in life and remain optimistic and motivated even in the face of adversity, Gail Sheehy writes,

> *"Even when pathfinders had an absent or severely flawed parent—-and many of them did—somewhere they found a person who became a transformative figure for them...Instead of allowing a less than ideal set of parents to set them back permanently, the potential pathfinders usually gravitated toward another figure who did have purpose and direction and who offered something healing, cohering, possibly even inspiring."*

Think back over your life and remember who your mentors were. Think about the impact they had on you. Now think about who you could mentor, sponsor, coach or teach. The only thing better than having a good mentor is being a good mentor!

—If you hear a voice within you saying "You are not a painter," then by all means paint...and that voice will be silenced.
—Vincent Van Gogh

Sprint to the Finish Line with Coaches

Successful people discover a way of drawing from the environment what they need. They find supporters who can help them overcome obstacles and can serve as coaches and cheerleaders. A good coach will provide a sense of structure in a person's life, thereby enabling them to take risks and make important changes. Forming a supportive partnership with a good coach provides reinforcement for your ideas and helps to keep you moving forward in the pursuit of your goals.

Working with a coach can help you to move through the steps to your goals more rapidly. A good example is Tiger Woods. Although he has a strong support system, he has four coaches; golf related and psychological/motivational. What top athletes have discovered is that their "inner game" is as important (if not more so) than their "outer game." Therefore, you need coaching for both.

Here are two more "pots of gold" for you: performance coaches and life coaches.

"Performance coaches" are experts in your field, who assist you with improving your physical skills. "Life coaches" who may know nothing about your field, can assist you with improving your mental performance. Life coaches can also be called "professional coaches," "personal coaches," "empowerment coaches," etc. Most top performers now have both types of coaches that they rely on. A coach's specialized training can provide structure and additional support, give you guidance and assess your progress along the way.

One of a coach's most important functions is to make you accountable for your progress. As you have learned in the chapter on goal setting, you will have mini-steps or sub-goals to accomplish on your way to your larger goal. Much like your teachers in school who gave you deadlines for turning in your homework, the coach should also give you time lines for achieving your sub-goals. This accountability can often be an important motivator in itself. Accountability can be provided by a mentor, spouse, employer, etc., but in a case where a support system is lacking, a coach may provide the necessary tools to keep your momentum going.

—The will to win is not nearly as important as the will to prepare to win.
—Unknown

Exercise 16:1
Changing Invalidation to Validation

1. Refer back to the exercise you did in Chapter 12, "Who Supports Me?" Make a list of at least 10 statements and/or actions that you can remember when someone invalidated, criticized, belittled or negated you throughout your life.

2. Now, change each statement or action into a validating one.

—Learn from the mistakes of others. We can't live long enough to make all of them ourselves.

—Unknown

Exercise 16:2
My Board of Directors

Imagine you have your very own "Invisible Board of Directors." There is a large conference table in the middle of a room. It is a large corner office in a sky rise office building with walls of glass and gorgeous views. There are 10 chairs around the table. You are at the head of the table. You can put anyone you want in the chairs. They can be people you know or don't know, dead or alive. Name the person who will sit in each chair. Choose the people you think would be your best supporters, have your best interest at heart, and give you the best advice.

For example, my Board of Directors consists of my deceased mother and father, my step-father, my best friend Victoria, my attorney, my gynecologist, my sister Anne, Oprah Winfrey, Wayne Dyer and God.

Any time you have a problem or concern, bring up your board of directors for a meeting. Imagine you are telling them about your problem. Imagine what each of them would say as you went around the table. You'll be surprised at what comes up!

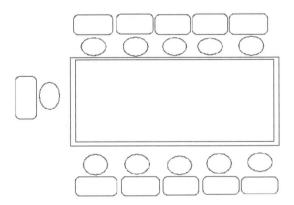

Chapter Seventeen:
Spiritual Aspects of Motivation

Finding Your Purpose

Your purpose will evolve over time. I have read every one of Wayne Dyer's books, and have noticed an evolution over the years. As Dyer has evolved as a person, his writing has reflected his deeper, more authentic person. His first books were mostly about managing your emotions, knowing that you are the product of whatever thoughts that you have, and becoming the kind of person you want to be. A few years later his message was more about not being a victim, not letting other people manipulate you, and taking responsibility for your own circumstances. A few years later he wrote more about self-actualization, fulfillment, joy and living at the highest level to which a human being can live. A few years later he began talking more about the process of enlightenment, peace and transformation. Most recently his teachings have taken on a more spiritual nature—the power of our intentions and our divine inspirations. I look forward to where he goes from here!

Brian Tracy, a well known motivational speaker says that he was able to turn his life around in a dramatic way once he had a "magnificent obsession." A "magnificent obsession" is when you dedicate your life to a powerful and compelling cause.

Doing "who you are" means living your true purpose, desires and gifts. This is where true fulfillment happens. Examples of people who are doing who they are:

**Oprah Winfrey—Oprah is often asked why she keeps signing three to five year contracts with Kingworld to keep her long-time award winning talk show going. She is often asked when she is going to get a "life." Her reply is always something like, "The show is my life, it is who I am, it is my gift. Why would I want to give that up?"

**Steven Spielberg—After creating a number of blockbuster movie hits such as E.T., Jaws, Jurrasic Park, The Color Purple, etc., Director Spielberg was snubbed by the Oscar Academy (except for an honoary Irving B. Thalberg Award). He had always wanted to create a movie about the Holocaust and had held the rights to author Thomas Keneally's Holocaust book for a decade. He had been discouraged from doing this movie as others felt it would be too "depressing" and not "commercial" enough. When Spielberg started his own family in the 80's, it rekindled an interest in his Jewish roots and sparked his decision to make the movie anyway. In 1994, *Schindler's List* brought him golden Oscar statues for Best Director and Best Picture (it swept seven in all).

**Mel Gibson—After spending $25 million of his own money to produce his movie *The Passion of the Christ*, Gibson was fired on by critics. The movie sparked more public controversy than any other movie of its kind. But Gibson was undaunted. His passion for making this film was greater than his fear of criticism. It turned out to be the number one box office hit of the year.

—Authentic empowerment is the knowing that you are on purpose, doing God's work, peacefully and harmoniously.

—Wayne Dyer

Hope Is a Thing With Feathers

Hope means that anything is possible. Anything you can dream, you can realize. Anything you set out to do, you can do. Hope is essential for life. Sometimes we are faced with situations that seem hopeless, yet they never are. I have found in my own life, and in the lives of many of my clients, that the antidote for depression is action.

Even after a tragedy we do not need to succumb to despair. By focusing on what you need to do in the NOW, or immediate future, i.e., get some sleep, pray, sit and sob; you are assuming a future. Even if your future only encompasses what you will do in the next hour, it is important to decide on what you can do now to get through it.

In the wake of a catastrophe it often feels impossible to summon the least glimmer of hope, faith or sense of life's meaning. Hope follows action and action follows hope. Making plans in the middle of a crisis doesn't change the crisis but changes your feelings about it. It gives you a small measure of control when your life feels out of control. Each step you take on your road map to recovery is a step born of hope. Each step then creates more hope. Soon you will have built a place where hope can nest.

Throughout history (before psychotherapy) people have found relief and comfort in the immediate obligations and habits of ordinary, daily life. Talking about practical, immediate plans calmed people down during crises. Focusing on mundane tasks in the present can help build, inch by inch and then yard by hard, a pathway out of despair and into the fullness of life. The simplest act can have profound healing power. If you cannot come up with what to do next, ask for advice from a trusted friend, family member, therapist or coach.

Hope is extremely important on your path to achieving your goals. Hope is what will keep you moving, working, completing daunting tasks, and trying new things. It is what keeps you stepping forward. Hold on to hope. Keep your vision of what your life will look like when you have achieved your goals. Do not worry so much about the "how-to's." The "how-to's" will work themselves out. Just take one step at a time toward your vision.

—*Hope is the thing with feathers…That perches on the soul…And sings the tune without the words…And never stops—at all.*
—Emily Dickinson

"When—Then" Syndrome—
How to Live NOW

Object relations theory is about our attachment to people, places, things, and/or events. I remember at a very young age thinking that once I had that thing I wanted, then, and only then, would I be happy. Most of us learned this in our childhoods, especially if we came from high achieving parents in the Western culture. I learned it from my parents, my teachers, my friends, the media, television, and just about everyone I knew. Unfortunately, we have very few role models who tell us otherwise.

When we attach our happiness or well being to an external object, or an "it" as I call it, (boyfriend, car, house, husband, child, ideal weight, etc.) we can never really be happy. My family gave me the message that I needed to marry "it." So I tried that, and it didn't work. They also gave me the message that my value lied mainly in what I could do for others. So I tried that, and it didn't work. They also gave me the message that I needed to do "it." So I did, and did, and did, and "it" didn't work. I followed all the other societal messages, constantly trying to "have it," "get it," "be it," and "hold onto it." I found myself running around like a crazy person—doing, getting, striving—doing, getting, striving. Yes, I did achieve many lofty goals that have brought me a great deal of satisfaction and pride. However, much of the time I was frustrated, stressed and exhausted. It didn't need to be so hard.

The problem with attaching ourselves to "its" is that once we get "it," we may be happier for a while, but then we must find a new "it" because we don't know how to just "be." It is like eating food. It satiates us for awhile, but we will get hungry again soon. When that "it" that we worked so hard for turns around and disappoints us, we are often more unhappy than before we got "it."

Achieving goals is a good thing. Having hope for a better life is a good thing. Striving toward our dreams is a good thing. But it becomes a bad thing when we are overly attached to these things. Once they do come into our lives, they don't "fill us up" the way we thought they would because we cannot be "filled up" (or fulfilled) with external things. We can only be truly "filled up" (or fulfilled) with ourselves.

What does this mean, being "filled up with ourselves?" Isn't that selfish and egotistical? I was taught not to be self centered. Family and society told me that I should be care more about others than I do about myself. I know they meant well, but they were wrong. Being "filled up with ourselves" is not about being self centered. It is about attaching to ourselves. It is about finding our true self, our core, our soul, our gifts, our desires, our needs, our passions. It is about getting to know who we are, deep down. It is about being our own best friend. It is about being happy, satisfied, and fulfilled with our "beingness." It is a spiritual pursuit, a journey into ourselves, or one could say, knowing the "God" within us.

—The happiest people seem to be those who have no particular reason for being happy except that they are so.

—W.R. Inge

Visualize Your Desired Outcome

Guided imagery, visualization, and hypnosis have shown to be very effective in motivational training. The "vision" (or image) one might create is how one's life will look when he/she has achieved one's goals. One could also create the vision of performing well at a desired skill. There can be many "visions" representing different aspects, or stages of the goal, however, the most effective vision is where you envision the *result* you desire. Another, more concrete method of using visualization, is to put pictures that represent your "vision" in conspicuous places around your home, car, computer, appointment book, etc. Saturating yourself with your vision of your goal attainment can help motivate you and keep you on track.

In sports motivation, Richard Suinn, Ph.D., sports psychologist, teaches his clients skills such as stress management, self-regulation, visualization, goal-setting, concentration, focus, and even relaxation (1999). He has written about a technique he calls "mental practice," which is also referred to as "visualization" or "imagery rehearsal." "It's the mental equivalent of physical practice," says Suinn. There is research evidence that indicates that when athletes use visualization after relaxation, their performance improves. The converse also holds true, if they imagine themselves doing poorly their performance worsens. Visualization works by bringing subconscious mental and emotional patterns into consciousness.

For example, a 50-year-old man wants to play baseball again. He decides to go to a baseball camp where he can play with the pros for a week. This man suffers from arthritis in his hip and does not want to take medication during his camp. Before going to his baseball camp, the man visualizes himself "playing baseball, feeling limber and free." In minute detail he fantasizes his movement, his performance, his emotional experience, exactly as he wants it to be. He sees and feels himself a winner. The man proceeds to have a wonderful time at camp and experience no pain while playing baseball.

Picture the fulfillment of your goals: see it, hear it, smell it, touch it, taste it. Think about what your life will be like when the goals are completed, what will be different and how you will feel. Afterwards, describe the picture in writing.

—*One of the best ways to recognize your strengths is to replay the tapes on your mind's "video player" of the times you were successful. Go back to any and all successful experiences: a big sale; a good grade at school; a winning performance in the orchestra, the band, or athletics; a great shot on the golf course or tennis court; a time when you and your family experienced a feeling of love and togetherness; an event when you were recognized for exceptional performance. Focus on one time in particular and recapture the sights, smells, and feelings that accompanied success. The next time you feel self-doubt creeping up on you, replay this vivid, positive tape.*

—Zig Ziglar

Positive Affirmations are Your Magic Words

Affirmations are powerful expressions of thought that many people have found to have amazing impact on realizing their desires. Our thoughts create our power. Because every thought has creative power, the more you think a thought, the more powerful it becomes. The more passion behind your thought, the more motion goes into the thought and the faster it manifests. In *The Game of Life and How to Play It*, Florence Shinn (1980) writes, "Our thoughts, actions and words return to us sooner or later with astounding accuracy. The idea, then, is to think only on what one wants, and not dwell on what one does not want."

Many people ask a "higher power" for their desires to come true. If this has been helpful to you I encourage you to continue. Another idea, less explicitly religious, is to make "grateful" affirmations, such as, "Thank you for giving me the intelligence and skill to succeed in my commercial art business," and "Thank you for bringing me two new clients today."

I believe that our desires are within us for a reason—a part of a divine plan. Thus there is no need to ask for things but rather to give thanks for them and know that one's desire is on its way. The following pages are examples of positive affirmations. Feel free to write some of your own! You can record your own affirmations onto audio CD or cassette and listen to them over and over. Repetition is one of the master keys to learning. The more you state positive affirmations, the less you will state negatives, as the positives will eventually squeeze out the negatives.

—Our lives are what our thoughts create.

—Wayne Dyer

Positive Affirmations

1. Dissolving Fear and Worry

I can handle my fears.
I am secure with myself.
My fears serve to protect me but do not control me.
I trust the universe is working for me and wants me to succeed.
Today I am free of fear and worry.
Today I am free of blame and guilt.
I am poised and speak with a strong, steady voice.
Things go my way.
Life is good to me.
I am calm and confident.

2. Overcoming Fear of Rejection

I am free of the fear of rejection by others.
I conquer fear of failure and criticism.
There are no failures, only learning experiences.
I am strong and self-assured.
I refuse to be limited by others' opinions.
I believe in myself.
I do not need to be all things to all people.
I attract healthy, supportive encouraging people in my life.
My opinions, feelings, thoughts, and ideas are valuable.
I have a high regard for others and they have a high regard for me.
I approve of myself.

3. Overcoming Obstacles

I have relaxed control of my life.
I have the toughness and determination to get through anything.
My nature is to stick with my plan and modify it only when necessary.
I meet challenges with composure and confidence.
Persistence is the key to my success.
I am increasing my inner strengths and abilities.
This situation is teaching me something I need to learn.
I know I will achieve great things.
I look at problems as challenges and find their solutions quickly and easily.
I am getting stronger each day.
I am in control of my life.

4. Positivity and Optimism

I am optimistic about my future.
I am confident about my life.
I am dedicated to my goals.
I know I am going to do something great.
I look at each task as a stepping stone to my success.
My clear-thinking mind generates new ideas for positive direction.
I have increasing tolerance for others' shortcomings.
I grow increasingly happy and fulfilled as I move toward my goals.
I feel great.
I am excited about my life.
I am at peace with who I am.

5. Taking Control of My Life

I have a strong determination to succeed.
I persevere even under difficult circumstances.
I am self-disciplined.
I am in control of myself and my life.
I confidently achieve my aims.
I am calm and relaxed in mind and body.
I take full responsibility for my life and the way I live it.
I can accomplish anything I set my mind to.
When things around me seem out of control, I know I can control myself.
I am strong and determined.

6. Enthusiasm and Motivation

I believe strongly in myself and in my dreams.
I have a lot of energy with which to accomplish my goals.
I am self motivated.
Whatever I do is done with enthusiasm and confidence.
I am cheerful and positive about life.
I am internally motivated to achieve my goals.
I finish all the projects I start.
I move forward from one accomplishment to the next.
I take great pride in achieving my goals.
I am a doer and a winner.
I am confident.
I feel good about myself.

7. Setting and Achieving Goals

I set goals that I can attain.
I write my goals down and review them daily to see my progress.
I am a high achiever.
I have a specific plan for my accomplishments.
I am not afraid of success or failure.
When I set a goal, I find a way to accomplish it.
My mind focuses on my goal until it is completed.
I enjoy the process of achieving my goals.
Obstacles may slow me down but will not prevent me from reaching my goals.
I can achieve whatever I set my mind on.
I can achieve whatever I believe in.

8. Start the Day Feeling Great!

I am grateful for the wonderful experiences that await me today.
Today brings fresh opportunities for fulfillment and happiness.
I eagerly look forward to whatever this day brings.
I am at peace with myself and the world around me.
I am grateful for my inner drive to accomplish my goals and enjoy life.
The energy I give out will flow back to me today.
I am grateful for my health and safety and the health and safety of my loved ones.
People respond positively to me today because I treat them with respect.
I attract good, happy, and satisfying experiences.
I greet the day with vitality and positive expectancy.
Today is a great day.

9. Finish the Day Feeling Great!

I feel good about my growth and learning today.
My life is secure and I am contented.
I am grateful for all that I have.
I dissolve all negativity in and around me.
I am free of blame and guilt.
I ask any questions I need answered and the answers will come.
I am a strong and enduring person.
My life is harmonious and fulfilling.
I am grateful for all the good and pleasant experiences in my life today.
I am grateful for the strength and endurance I had today.
Tomorrow is a new day to do things differently.
I choose to be contented with my life.
I have peace of mind.
I am grateful.

—Real-magic thinkers say, "I believe it, I know it, and I will access my spiritual powers to do it. It is my intention."

—Wayne Dyer

Exercise 17:1
Using Affirmations

Examples of Positive Affirmations:
1. My ideas are worth being taken seriously.
2. I have the right to pursue my dreams.
3. If I believe in my goals, I can make them happen.
4. I have the right to devote time to my own needs and yearnings.
5. I deserve happiness and fulfillment.

Write 10 Affirmations of your own:

1._____
2._____
3._____
4._____
5._____
6._____
7._____
8._____
9._____
10._____

> —We are what we think. All that we are arises with our thoughts.
> With our thoughts we make the world.
>
> —Buddha

Part IV:

HOW TO MOTIVATE OTHERS

Chapter Eighteen:
Motivating Others

The One Minute Motivational Technique that Works Better than Anything

Many books have been written on the subject of motivation, such as *The One Minute Manager* by Kenneth Blanchard and Spencer Johnson (1983) and many other books with the words "One Minute" in their title. "One minute" simply means that it only takes a minute or less to motivate someone to their fullest! The one minute motivational technique that works better than anything else is *validation*. Below are ways of validating people to get the most from them:

Saying (or writing) something positive about someone
Affirming them
Praising them
Complimenting them
Thanking them
Noticing them
Paying full attention to them
Listening to them
Empathizing with them
Understanding them

You will notice that none of these things takes more than a minute to do. You will notice that they are all fairly easy to do. When people are validated they feel valued and empowered. They also enjoy their work more when they are around positive people who pay attention to them. People want to *matter*. It is your job to make them feel that they matter. Be sure to focus just as much on the *person* and their *effort* as on their *results*. This is so easy to do that it is amazing that most people hardly ever do it! It is SO worth the time and energy. Try it for a few days. You will be amazed by what happens!

—*I can live for two months on a good compliment.*

—Mark Twain

How to Motivate Others

The theory of the "Dipper and the Bucket" was created by Tom Rath and Donald Clifton (2004) and explained in their book *How Full is Your Bucket?* They explain the theory this way: "Each of us has an invisible bucket. It is constantly emptied or filled, depending on what others say or do to us. When our bucket is full, we feel great. When it's empty, we feel awful. Each of us also has an invisible dipper. When we use that dipper to fill other people's buckets—by saying or doing things to increase their positive emotions—we also fill our own bucket. But when we use that dipper to dip from others' buckets—by saying or doing things that decrease their positive emotions—we diminish ourselves. Like the cup that runneth over, a full bucket gives us a positive outlook and renewed energy. Every drop in that bucket makes us stronger and more optimistic. But an empty bucket poisons our outlook, saps our energy, and undermines our will. That's why every time someone dips from our bucket, it hurts us. So we face a choice every moment of every day: We can fill one another's buckets, or we can dip from them. It's an important choice—one that profoundly influences our relationships, productivity, health and happiness."

The same basic techniques seem to work well for all people. Validation and recognition are the best ways to motivate anyone. I have discussed throughout this book the important role of social reinforcement. People want to be noticed. When you notice people for doing good, they want to keep doing good. This is because social validation moves people from a feeling of a minus to a feeling of a plus. This being said, sometimes social validation can be destructive, as in the case of a teenager getting involved in a gang. Obviously, someone in the gang showed interest in the teen and caused him/her to feel better. When children lack enough social reinforcement for doing positive things, they will often get caught up in the current of those who pay attention to them, even when they know those people are doing bad things. Sometimes even children who have had lots of social reinforcement for doing positive things get caught in the web of destructive people. This is why it is extremely important that children are taught from an early age how important it is to choose people wisely. Parents need to help their children make good choices in friends as long as it is humanly possible.

One technique that works very well with friends, family and children is the "What I Want for You" technique. You simply state to the person, "What I want for you is…" Just make the statement and say nothing else. It is important that you stop talking here. Allow your words to soak in to the person and allow them to respond. If they do not respond, that's okay. Your words are in their mind and their memory. If they have a good relationship with you, your words will matter—maybe not now—but eventually.

—Soft words are hard arguments.

—Thomas Fuller

How to Motivate Kids

Everyone is born with ambition. Just spend a few minutes with a baby learning to walk or a headstrong toddler learning to talk. No matter how many times young children stumble and fall, almost all of them keep on trying. Children are very determined creatures. Mastering a new skill is the highlight of their day. That being said, it is unfortunate that somewhere around puberty, a good number of kids seem to lose their natural drive to succeed. Somewhere around the start of middle school many kids become under-achievers. For high achieving parents, whose own ambition is often tied to their children's success, this can be a very difficult and painful time.

Kids can be given opportunities to become passionate about a subject or activity, but they cannot be forced. Figuring out where, when and why the fire went out is the first step to reigniting the fire. First look at extinguishers such as family crises, emotional distress or learning disabilities. The most common flame snuffers however, are fear of failure and peer pressure. The kind of peer pressure that puts out fires is the message that doing something really well academically, athletically, or artistically is just "not cool." Some experts say our education system puts too much emphasis on testing, thereby segregating kids according to ability, which places too much pressure on youngsters. All kids are gifted in some way. However, schools do not focus on each child's unique gift, but rather examine only their ability to perform well on certain tests.

Carol Dweck, a psychology professor at Stanford (Kluger, 2005), helped run an experimental workshop with New York City public school seventh-graders to teach them that they are in charge of their intellectual growth (not their parents, teachers or peers). "The message is that everything is within the kids' control, that their intelligence is malleable," says Lisa Blackwell, a research scientist at Columbia University who worked with Dweck to develop and run the program. The result of the project was that the students' interest in school increased and turned around their declining math grades. "Parents can play a critical role in conveying this message to their children by praising their effort, strategy and progress rather than emphasizing their 'smartness' or praising high performance alone. Most of all, parents should let their kids know that mistakes are a part of learning."

Remember that pressure creates resistance. Just like the lid of a pressure cooker that wants to blow off, so too will kids want to "blow you off." Talk to children as you would talk to adults (while toning down your vocabulary to words they can understand). Be careful not to lecture them. Controlling and dominating result in the exact opposite of motivating others. When people sense you are dominating, they will not only tune you out but will resist and/or oppose whatever you are saying.

When dealing with kids, the most important thing to remember is to praise the *effort*, not the *results*. Once they get a spark, they will be able to use their effort to keeps its flame burning. Effort is what fuels motivation and ambition. When kids hit a wall where they feel the effort is too much and they want to quit, ask them to remember times in the past when they worked through a particularly difficult task. Ask them to tell you how it felt to have overcome the struggle and get to the desired result. Let them know they can do that same thing again, in new situations. Offer as many different experiences as possible, and look for the spark. Then fan its flame.

—The only place you find success before work is in the dictionary.
—May V. Smith

Lessons From a Butterfly

There is a story about a man who found a cocoon of a butterfly. One day he noticed a small opening appeared in the cocoon. He sat and watched the butterfly for several hours as it struggled to force its body through that little hole. Then it seemed to stop making any progress. It appeared as if it had gotten as far as it could and it could go no further. So, the man decided to help the butterfly. He took a pair of scissors and snipped off the remaining bit of the cocoon. The butterfly emerged easily. But, it had a swollen body, and small shriveled wings. He continued to watch the butterfly, because he expected that, at any moment, the wings would enlarge and expand to support the body, which would contract in time. Neither happened. In fact, the butterfly spent the rest of its life crawling around with a swollen body and shriveled wings. It was never able to fly. What the man did not understand was that the restricting cocoon and the struggle required to get through the tiny opening was nature's way of forcing fluid from the body of the butterfly into its wings so that it would be ready for flight once it achieved its freedom from the cocoon.

Sometimes struggles are exactly what we need in our life. If we went through life without any obstacles or frustrations, we would never learn how to endure, and would therefore be crippled. As hard as it is to watch your loved ones go through struggles, we have to be very careful and thoughtful before trying to rescue them or fix their problems. Motivation often comes from our successes; particularly those that were hard fought and won. Unless it is absolutely necessary, do not deny others that kind of success.

—The harder I worked the luckier I got. If you're that focused you're going to ultimately achieve what you want to do.
—Jon Bon Jovi

New Ways to Motivate Employees

The old "command and control" style of management is passé. Nowadays, employees want "perks." And the two main perks employees state that they want are (no, not more money!) 1) more time communicating with upper management, and 2) more recognition.

According to the U.S. Department of Labor, the number one reason people leave their jobs is because they "do not feel appreciated." Yet praise seems to be rare in the workplace. Numerous studies show that most employees are never praised or complimented at work. One poll found that an astounding 65% of Americans reported receiving no recognition for good work in the past year. Further studies show that recognition and praise are two of the best ways to motivate others at work. A study by Rath and Clifton (2004) that included more than 4 million employees worldwide, found that individuals who receive regular recognition and praise:

- Increase their individual productivity
- Increase engagement among their colleagues
- Are more likely to stay with their organization
- Receive higher loyalty and satisfaction scores from customers
- Have better safety records and fewer accidents on the job.

Therefore, one of the most crucial things you can do to motivate people at work is to simply praise, recognize or compliment them.

One of the fine arts of management is the ability to show interest in subordinates. The best way to do this is by showing your personal interest in their projects and their jobs, checking on progress, and being quick to help in any way you can. There is no substitute for interest. Things that you are obviously interested in tend to get done first and on time. If you show little interest, jobs may get done later—or perhaps not at all. While employees may not always be interested in what they are doing, by you showing interest, they will likely become interested in turn.

The famous management consultants Tom Peters and Nancy Austin (2004) studied a number of successful companies in an attempt to discover the secret of their success. The management technique they found most common to these successful companies was something they call MBWA—Management by Walking Around. Instead of staying behind their desks in a private office, the most successful managers were constantly moving around the establishment, talking with customers, employees, and anyone else who might give them a new insight into how to make the business better.

Some progressive companies have instituted ways of recognizing employees such as "Employee of the Month." However, more recent studies have shown that these types of awards do not have as much meaning as simply saying, "You made a difference today," or "Thank you for getting our accounting in order with XYZ Company. I really appreciate your efforts on that project." Generic, one-size-fits-all awards don't work. Neither does recognition that seems forced or fake. Whatever recognition and praise you provide must have meaning that is specific to each individual.

Sometimes managers and supervisors have to be critical or confront problems with employees. When this is necessary, be sure to follow the "four-to-one" rule. For every criticism you make of someone's job performance, make sure you give the person four compliments. At the very least, employ the "sandwich" rule. First give a compliment, then a criticism, then another compliment. When an employee does not seem to be able to grasp his/her job, see if they would fit better with another job. Remember the old saying, "Never try to teach a pig to sing. It wastes your time and it annoys the pig."

—Perpetual optimism is a force multiplier.

—Colin Powell

The Four Magical Words to Deal With Resistance

There are people who have a negative view of themselves and the world. I call these people "impossibility thinkers." No matter what idea you present to them, they always find ways to justify why it won't work. They really do not want to change. They really do not want to do anything. They may *say* they want their lives to be better, and they may *complain* endlessly about how bad it is, but they will never let you help them find a solution.

When you attempt to help people who do not want to be helped, they will often "turn" on you. The easiest way to justify not doing anything is to discount the messenger. They may think that "the messenger is no good" therefore their message is invalid, therefore I don't have to do anything. If you notice that you are trying to motivate, help, aid, assist someone who will not take any of your good advice, you need to realize that you will soon be dealing with someone who MUST disrespect you and MUST make you out to be the "bad guy." It is their only method of resisting you.

Therapy offices are full of resistant people. It is my opinion that most clients could avoid seeking therapy if they would just take the good advice of their family and friends. This means asking at least ten people in your life who you know care about you, what they would suggest you do in a dilemma. Usually you will get a "common thread" of good advice that stands out. Yet many people are stubborn and rebellious, or prefer to find out things on their own, in their own way, as discussed in Chapter Eleven: I Have to Do It My Way.

Some people are covertly resistant. We call this "passive resistance" or "passive aggression." For example, when you ask your son to take out the garbage and he says he will, but then "forgets" to do it, he is being passive resistant. The way to deal with this is to give people time limits with directives. If they do not do it within the allotted time frame, you need to calmly confront it and have a discussion about it. Set up a plan that both you and the other person can agree to in order to solve the problem.

When someone is chronically resistant, defiant or oppositional, it may not be possible to turn them around. However, if they are simply passively resistant now and then, there are strategies you can use to motivate them. One strategy that has already been mentioned is praise and validation when they are doing something good, or at least putting in a good effort. Another strategy is to say, "I need your help." These are the magical words with the greatest persuasive powers. "I need help" doesn't have the same impact as "I need *your* help." The word "*your*" is what gives the phrase clout because it makes the words personal. It is very difficult to say "no" to someone who comes right out and asks for *your* assistance. This phrase comes in handy when people really don't want to be helpful (like my teenage daughter).

—The giant oak is an acorn that held its ground.

—Anonymous

Don't Fix, Coach!

Most people who desire change can benefit greatly by coaching from someone who they admire and respect. The definition of coaching is: *assisting people with goal achievement.* Just know that coaching only works with people who truly want assistance. Even if the person is not very motivated, all they need is a desire and willingness to start a step-by-step process. The type of coaching I'm discussing here can be called many different names, such as: life coaching, personal coaching, motivational coaching, performance coaching, empowerment coaching, etc. The coach's job is to provide the following:

- Structure
- A road map
- Support for challenges and obstacles
- Validation
- Encouragement

Note that the coach's job is not to fix, or enable, or do for others what they can do for themselves. It is simply to provide guidance and step-by-step instructions so that the person has someone to be accountable to. Some people simply need to know they have a cheerleader behind them. Professional athletes and other celebrities often say that their fans motivate them tremendously. You can be that fan for someone.

I have been a professional coach for over a decade, and I can't tell you how rewarding it is. Clients often tell me that coaching was the best thing they ever did for themselves. They often tell me that this was the first time anyone ever really showed interest in helping them achieve their goals, not to mention support, validation and encouragement!

Each individual has his/her own "greatness potential." Coaching is a way of drawing that greatness out of the person. It is an alliance—a team effort—both coach and coachee working together in a co-creative process. It is an opportunity for you to empower others to become all they can be.

There are many good professional coach training programs available. You don't need to be professionally trained to help someone out here or there for no fee, but I recommend you take a few classes or read a few books on coaching before you attempt to actually coach someone. Even if you are providing coaching for no fee, you have an obligation to be competent at what you are doing. As in any relationship, there is potential for harm. Providing coaching is an art and a skill that needs to be learned and practiced.

—Enthusiasm is one of the most powerful engines of success. When you do a thing, do it with all your might…Be active, be energetic, be enthusiastic and faithful, and you will accomplish your objective.
—Ralph Waldo Emerson

Enthusiasm is Contageous

Enthusiasm is like a powerful magnet that compels people to want to stop and listen. If you have a clear vision that you're genuinely excited about, people will be attracted to you, because unfortunately, most people don't have one. When you are really excited about your goal or dream, people walking by will want to stop and listen in—without even knowing what you're talking about—just because they are attracted and curious about your enthusiasm.

The word "enthusiasm" translates to "the God within." Therefore, if you have a dream that is truly "you" it will automatically create enthusiasm within you. If your dream or goal does not bring up a feeling of excitement, passion or enthusiasm, it is probably not really "you." It is possible to create enthusiasm in others simply by helping them to know what they really want. The best supervisor I ever had at work often asked me questions like, "What do you want, Lyn? What do you want out of life? What do you really want to do? How would your job look if it were exactly how you wanted it?" Not only did her questions make me feel that she was interested in me as a person, they really made me think bigger about what I really wanted. They made me think more about who I was and what worked or didn't work for me. They also gave me hope that perhaps I could actually get some of the things in my life that I truly desired. She was the most motivating boss I ever had.

—You can do anything if you have enthusiasm.

—Henry Ford

Exercise 18:1
How Good am I at Motivating Others?

Answer true or false to the following statements. If you would like more objective feedback, ask a close friend or family member to rate you!

I have praised or complimented someone today.

I focus on the positive with others.

I have a knack for making other people feel good.

I give more positive statements to others than negative statements.

I am more positive than negative in my conversations in general.

I make it a point to get to know people I've just met by showing general interest in them.

I ask questions and spend more time listening to others than talking about myself.

I can make people laugh.

I make it a point to say something nice to each person I encounter each day.

I notice when others go above and beyond the call of duty, and tell them so.

When I am upset, frustrated or angry with someone, I wait until I have calmed down before confronting them.

Whenever I have to give negative feedback to someone, I always sandwich it with positives.

People often say they feel good around me.

People often thank me for helping them or doing something nice for them.

I often do "anonymous good." I do something for someone without telling them or anyone else.

People generally feel I am on their side.

I do not give advice unless I am asked.

I focus on being *interested* rather than *interesting*.

—*"Come to the edge," he said. They said, "we are afraid." "Come to the edge," he said. They came. He pushed them. And they flew.*
                                                        —Guillaume Apollinaire

Conclusion
Accepting Your Success

Get Over Your Fear of Success

Many of us will need to be able to motivate ourselves most of the time. There will not always be a cheerleader in our midst. One way you can keep your motivation strong is to take time periodically to relax and appreciate your hard work and effort. Take time and energy for yourself, to do something just for you. If you have been working lots of hours, reward yourself with some time off to do something you enjoy. If you have been dieting for weeks and finally lost that ten pounds, reward yourself by going to your favorite restaurant or buying yourself a new outfit. After finishing each chapter of this book I rewarded myself with a day off of writing doing something fun. I might get a massage, go to a movie, go to a concert or comedy show, rent some videos, go shopping, plant some flowers, or just read a good book all day. After I finish writing this book I'm going to take a mini-vacation to relax and have fun.

Above all, savor each success along the way. It really is more about the journey than the destination. Completion of each step, each task, each item on your list of things to do needs to be congratulated by YOU! Each step along the way puts you that much closer to your goal. And achieving your goal feels FABULOUS! Accept your success! You've earned it!

In the past, when I would achieve something great, I would often feel afraid of losing it. This was because having the success was something I was not comfortable with yet. It takes time to feel secure and comfortable with the changes your success creates. Allow yourself this time to let it sink in. Do not allow your fear of losing it to rob you of your joy of gaining it. Trust yourself to handle your success in a noble fashion and not flitter it away. Trust the Universe that it is working for your highest good.

Your path to your dream is paved with sacrifices and lined with determination. Your path will have many stumbling blocks along the way, and may veer off in many different directions. It is traveled by faith, belief, courage, persistence and hard work. It is conquered with a willingness to face challenges and take chances, and fail and try again and again. You may have many doubts, setbacks and unfairness along the way. But when your path comes to its destination, you will find that there is no greater joy than making your dream come true.

Enjoy your success—you've earned it! I wish you much happiness and joy in your journey toward making your (and others') dreams come true.

—Fortune's expensive smile is earned.

—Emily Dickenson

Exercise 19:1
Motivational Music Gets You Moving!

Music can inspire people to take action. It can actually increase adrenaline in your brain and give you more energy. Find out if it works for you. Try listening to different types of music and see if there is a particular sound that motivates you and gets you excited. Some suggestions of music that many people find energizing and inspirational are:

— "I'm So Excited," *Pointer Sisters Greatest Hits,* 1989 BMG Music.

— "One Moment in Time," Whitney Houston, *1988 Summer Olympics* Album, Arista.

— "Gonna Fly Now" (theme song), *Rocky, Original Motion Picture Score,* 1976, United Artists.

Write the names of music titles that motivate you:

Create a "Greatest Motivational Hits" tape or tape library for yourself. Listen to it frequently or whenever you need a "lift."

—There is one elementary truth, the ignorance of which kills countless ideas and splendid plans: that the moment one definitely commits oneself, the providence moves, too…Whatever you can do, or dream you can, begin it.

—Goethe

References

Bandura, Albert. (1977) *Social learning theory.* Englewood Cliffs, NJ: Prentice Hall.

Blanchard Kenneth and Johnson, Spencer. (1983) *The one minute manager.* Berkeley Trade.

Bliss, Edwin. (1986) *Doing it now.* New York: Simon & Schuster.

Boggiano, Ann K. and Pittman, Thane S. (Eds.). (1992) *Achievement and motivation.* New York: Cambridge University Press.

Braham, Barbara. (1999) *Finding your purpose.* Crisp Publications, Menlo Park, CA.

Breathnach, Sarah. (1995) *Simple abundance.* New York: Warner Books.

Brounstein, Marty. (2001) *Coaching & mentoring for dummies.* IDG Books. New York, NY.

Brown, Les. (1992) *Live your dreams.* New York, NY: Avon Books, Inc.

Canfield, Jack and Victor Hanson, Mark. (1995) *The aladdin factor.* Berkeley, CA.

Carter, James J. (1989) *Nasty people.* Chicago, IL. Contemporary Books.

Chandler, Steve. (1996) *100 ways to motivate yourself.* High Bridge Co.

Chopra, Deepak, MD. (1995) *The seven spiritual laws of success.* Amber-Allen.

Deci, Edward L. (1985) *Intrinsic motivation and self-determination in human behavior.* New York: Plenum.

Douglas, John and Olshaker, Mark. (2000) *The anatomy of motive.* Scribner Publishing.

Dyer, Wayne. (1980) *The sky's the limit.* New York: Pocket Books.

Dyer, Wayne and Chopra, Deepak. (2003) *How to get what you really, really, really want.* Audiobook.

Epstein, Robert, Ph.D. (1999) Helping athletes go for the gold. *Psychology Today.* May/June, p.20.

Frankl, Victor. (1992) *Man's search for meaning.* Cutchogue, NY. Buccaneer Books.

Gawain, Shakti. (1995) *Creative visualization.* San Rafael, CA: New World Library.

Gollwitzer, Peter & Bargh, John A. (1996) *The psychology of action: linking cognition and motivation to behavior.* New York: Guilford Press.

Green, Russell G. (1995) *Human motivation: a social psychological approach.* Pacific Grove, CA: Brooks/Cole.

Hannig, Paul. (1997) Self-defeating personality disorder (SD): a profile. *The California Therapist.* Sept/Oct.

Heller, Sharon, Ph.D. (1999) *The complete idiot's guide to conquering fear and anxiety.* Alpha Books. New York, NY.

Hennessey, Beth A, & Amabile, Teresa M. (1998) Reality, intrinsic motivation, and creativity. *American Psychologist.* 53, 674–675.

Hill, Napolean, (1960) *Think and grow rich.* New York: Doubleday.

Hudson, Frederic M. (1999) *The handbook of coaching.* CA: Jossey-Bass Publishers.

Isaacs, Ernest. (1997) Taming the inner critic. *The California Therapist.* Sept./Oct.

Johnson, Spencer, M.D. (2000) *Who moved my cheese?* Putnam Publishing.

Kelley, Lyn. (2001) *How to motivate your clients to change.* San Diego, CA: GROW Publications.

Kluger, J. (2005) Ambition: why some people are most likely to succeed. *Time Magazine.* Nov. 14.

Maslow, Abraham. (1970) *Motivation and personality.* (2nd ed.). New York: Harper and Row.

O'Neil, Harold F., & Drillings, Michael. (Eds.). (1994) *Motivation: theory and research.* Hillsdale, NJ: L. Erlbaum Associates.

Pamplin, Robert B. (1993) *One who believed: true stories of faith.* Christ Community Church.

Peters, Tom and Robert Waterman. (2004) *In search of excellence.* Collins Books.

Prochaska, J.O., Norcross, J.C., and DiClimente, C.C. (1995) *Changing for good.* New York: Avon.

Rath, Tom and Clifton, Donald. (2004) *How full is your bucket?* Gallup Press. NewYork, NY.

Robbins, Anthony. (1991) *Unlimited power.* New York: Fawcett Books.

Rothman, Smith, Nakashima, Paterson, and Mustin. (1996) Client self-determination and professional intervention. *Social Work.* 41:4.

Scott, Steven K. (1998) *Simple steps to impossible dreams.* New York: Simon and Schuster.

Seligman, Martin E.P. (1990) *Learned helplessness.* New York, NY: A.A. Knopf.

Seligman, Martin E.P. (1994) *What you can change and what you can't.* New York: A.A. Knopf.

Sheehy, Gail. *Passages.* New York: Bantam.

Shinn, Florence. (1980) *The game of life and how to play it*. New York: Simon and Schuster.

Swinn, Richard. (1999) Helping athletes go for the gold. *Psychology Today*. May, p. 20.

Thomas, Marlo, and friends. (2002) *The right words at the right time*. New York: Atria books.

Tracy, Brian. (1997) *Secrets of success*.

Twerski, Abraham. (1997) *Life's too short!* New York: St. Martin's Griffin.

Viorst, Judith. (1998) *Imperfect control*. New York: Simon and Schuster.

Waitley, Denis. (1997) *The new dynamics of goal setting*. New York: William Morrow.

Winfrey, Oprah. (2002-2006) *O Magazine*. Various issues.

978-0-595-38002-2
0-595-38002-6

Made in the USA
Monee, IL
18 December 2019